The Globalization Trap

The Globalization Trap

Reclaiming American Prosperity

Michael Collins

BUSINESS EXPERT PRESS
Leader in applied, concise business books

The Globalization Trap: Reclaiming American Prosperity

Copyright © Business Expert Press, LLC, 2026.

Cover design by Gregory Paus

Interior design by S4Carlisle Publishing Services, Chennai, India

First published in 2026 by
Business Expert Press, LLC
222 East 46th Street, New York, NY 10017
www.businessexpertpress.com

ISBN-13: 978-1-63742-950-1 (paperback)
ISBN-13: 978-1-63742-951-8 (e-book)

Economics and Public Policy Collection

First edition: 2026

10 9 8 7 6 5 4 3 2 1

EU SAFETY REPRESENTATIVE
Mare Nostrum Group B.V.
Doelen 72
4831 GR Breda
The Netherlands
gpsr@mare-nostrum.co.uk

Contents

List of Tables and Figures

Tables

Figures

Acknowledgments

My greater debt of gratitude is due to my three friends—Pat O'Connor, Richard Armstrong, and Bill Huebner—who reviewed each chapter of the book over a 5-month period. Their many decades of manufacturing experience as well as their many comments and criticisms led to many changes that helped me weld together all of the ideas in this book.

Description

This book is based on three themes: the decline of the middle class, the failure of the service economy, and how we can reclaim prosperity.

Decline of the middle class—Milton Friedman was one of the founders of neoliberalism and he became famous when he said in a *New York Times* article that "An entity's greatest responsibility lies in the satisfaction of the shareholders." The doctrine of shareholder value put neoliberalism and globalism into overdrive as a new business philosophy for American multinational corporations (MNCs) and the government. It would have dire consequences for labor, unions, workers, and communities, and would be the driving force in the economy from 1980 to the present.

Perhaps the most important economic factor from the point of view of labor was that globalization and outsourcing caused regression to the mean (RTM), which pitted American workers against low wage workers around the world. RTM was a disaster for the American middle class, particularly workers with a high school diploma or less, it became a race to the bottom.

The failure of the service economy—Many economists and academics jumped on the "postindustrial service" bandwagon and have convinced themselves and most citizens that the transition to a service economy is a good and inevitable thing. These same economists also, believed that the service economy and cheap imported goods would provide economic growth, good jobs, and improved living standards for the middle class. But it just didn't happen for millions of workers.

If the transition to a service economy was such a good idea, you should ask yourself, *Why are so many people unhappy with their income and living standards and fearful of the future?* The price of cheap imported goods was not enough to offset the stagnant wages and rising living costs of most workers. The idea that we could rely on services to replace manufacturing and maintain living standards was an illusion. My argument is that continuing to depend on a service economy, the status quo, and a free trade policy based on cheap imports, is an economic pipe dream and could result in middle class rebellion.

Refloating the boats: how we can reclaim prosperity—rather than a single, interconnected network, globalization is fracturing. This fracturing is driven by the implementation of Trump's tariffs, political instability, the rise of protectionist policies, and reactive tariffs by foreign competitors, which are dividing the globalized world into separate trading blocs. The fracturing of globalization has provided an opportunity for a new industrial policy and plan that can reverse the decline of the middle class.

Is it still possible for the average worker to attain the American Dream, and can the decline of the middle class be reversed?" I didn't think so for many years when the big importers and outsourcing were running rampant.

To have a chance of creating an economy with wages rising faster than inflation, and rising living standards, we will have to abandon free trade and globalism, bring manufacturing back to the United States, reduce our trade deficit, and protect our industries and technologies. We will have to incentivize U.S. multinationals to stop outsourcing and incentivize both foreign and U.S. companies to establish manufacturing operations within the United States.

Trump's tariffs were a good first step in using tariffs to level the trading playing field and protect our manufacturing industries and technologies. But the real answer is not just a reliance on tariffs but to commit to production—not consumption—and use the elements of productivism to develop a comprehensive plan including dollar realignment.

Preface

From 1940 to 1980 the growth of the middle class increased with productivity growth and all boats rose with the tide. The old adage "a rising tide lifts all boats" used to apply to the American economy. It was a time when the American Dream was truly attainable by any American worker with determination.

According to Jeff Ferry of the Coalition for a Prosperous America (CPA),

"The strength of our manufacturing sector from 1870 to 1970, and its tendency to pay high wages to its workers was the single most important factor in national wealth and in our strong middle class. The aim of globalization from 1990 on, was to force US workers to compete with low wage workers around the world."

The resultant deindustrialization has led to the decline of the middle class, and sacrificing jobs, industries, technologies, suppliers, and communities.

Neoliberalism is an ideology that emphasizes globalism, free trade, and letting the markets regulate the economy. It is a unique form of libertarianism that includes:

- The privatization of state-owned enterprises like public schools, air traffic control, and programs like Social Security and Medicare
- Tax reduction for corporations and their shareholders
- Shrinking government in terms of workers and power
- National economies must be deregulated to give the markets and entrepreneurs a chance to do their magic

Neoliberalism was the theoretical foundation for radical economic changes and was closely connected to the strategy of outsourcing and globalization. It also began the slow hollowing of American industry called deindustrialization.

This book is about how neoliberalism and globalization were adopted by American Corporations and the U.S. government and how they radically changed the American economy and exploited the working class. The following were the major changes:

1. **Free Trade and Trade Agreements:** Most politicians, both Democrat and Republican, believed in free trade and that it would create jobs, boost overall trade (including exports), and give the United States access to foreign markets. To this end they pursued free trade agreements which led to the deindustrialization of America and the decline of the middle class.

2. **Outsourcing:** According to the Economic Policy Institute, American corporations have outsourced more than 5 million jobs and 91,000 plants since 1997[1] When it is easy to procure cheap imported goods, there is less pressure to raise domestic wages, and, in fact, there is pressure to reduce wages.

3. **Regression To the Mean:** Outsourcing caused Regression To the Mean (RTM) which pitted American workers against low wage workers around the world. The pressure from the mean puts pressure on the wages of the high wage country which over time reduces American wages closer to the mean of foreign wages. RTM was a disaster for the American middle class, and led to wage stagnation and wage reduction.

4. **The Losers:** All presidents, from Reagan to Biden, Republican and Democrat, supported free trade and globalization. The problem with economic theories like free trade and Globalization is that they always cover up or down play what happens to the losers. They knew there would be losers in free trade but believed that the benefits outweighed the downside. For millions of workers, free trade meant shifting them into low-wage jobs and the slide into economic oblivion.

5. **Middle Class Decline:** According to a Pew Research Center analysis of government data, the middle class has steadily contracted in the past five decades. The share of adults who live in middle-class

---

[1]Robert E. Scott, "Trump's Trade Policies Have Cost Thousands of U.S. Manufacturing Jobs," *Economic Policy Institute*, August 10, 2020.

households fell from 61 percent in 1971 to 50 percent in 2021, while its share of national income declined from 52 to 45 percent.

6. **Manufacturing Jobs:** Since 1980, America has lost more than 7.5 million manufacturing jobs in approximately 388 manufacturing industries.

7. **Union Membership:** Membership also declined from 53 to 10 percent from 1967 to 2014.

8. **Inequality:** The primary cause of rising inequality was economic globalization, free trade, tax reduction, and RTM. From 1970 to 2018, the share of aggregate income going to middle-class households fell from 62 to 43 percent (see Figure 2.4, Chapter 2). Over the same period, the share held by upper-income households increased from 29 to 48 percent.

9. **Deregulation of the Financial Industry:** In the late 1970s, when wages began to stagnate the middle class tried to keep up their buying power by women going to work, working longer hours, drawing down savings, and going into debt. As financial regulations slowly collapsed, Wall Street introduced predatory lending in the form of high-interest rate credit cards with fees and penalties, payday loans, and subprime mortgages. The middle class *tried to use debt as a substitute for income* to maintain a middle-class lifestyle.

10. **Inflation and Rising Prices:** Essential costs like health care, education, and housing have skyrocketed since 1980, squeezing the middle class and reducing living standards. Today, millions of middle-class citizens cannot buy a home, afford health care or afford to go to college.

11. **Tax Reduction:** The MNCs and their lobbyists were very successful in getting five tax reduction laws for corporations and their shareholders since 1981. The MNCs used most of their new profits to buy back shares of their own stock to increase the share price and realize more short-term profits.

12. **Monopolies and Oligopolies:** Since 1999 the United States has undergone an enormous number of mergers and acquisitions, mostly by large corporations. Mutinational Corproations (MNC) have formed monopolies and oligopolies in industries like the airlines, big banks, hospitals, meat packers. media companies, beer, autos, and oil and gas. It gave them the power to control

employment, wages, supply chains, consumer pricing, and market share. Antitrust actions died with the Reagan administration.

13. **Globalization and Free Trade:** It became a one-sided process where the benefits would flow to capital and the costs to labor. Neoliberalism and globalization were a godsend for the 1 percent whose wealth had an incredible increase in their percentage of national income—a growth of 162 percent since 1980.

14. **Backlash:** There was a middle-class backlash, which was very evident in the 2024 presidential election, when the middle class voted their pocketbook.

My conclusion is that globalization and the rise of neoliberalism as a political ideology turned out to be a trap where the average middle-class citizen bore the brunt of the economic changes through job losses, stagnant wages, and not being able to keep up with inflation. Economic inequality has led to social, political, economic division, and polarization, making it harder for society to function and poses the threat of future instability. A shrinking middle-class has also led to widespread economic hardship which has led to anger, resentment, frustration, and a sense of no future. Unless the country can provide improved living standards, higher wages, and reduced inequality there is a risk of political extremism and nondemocratic radical solutions.

The best summary of the fallacy of the postindustrial service economy was summarized by Harold Myerson in *The Washington Post*. He said,

"The Wall Street/Wal-Mart economy of the past several decades off-shored millions of factory jobs, which it offset by creating low-paying jobs in the service and retail sectors: extending credit to consumers so they could keep consuming despite their stagnating incomes; and fueling, until it collapsed, a boom in construction."

He also writes that

"of all the lies that the American people have been told in the past four decades, the biggest one may be this: We'll all come out ahead in the shift from an industrial to post-industrial society.

The post-industrial economy turned out to be a bust. The time for neo-industrial America has arrived."

The good news is that both neoliberalism and globalization are in decline. Globalization is fracturing, meaning the world economy is splintering into distinct blocs, rather than a single, interconnected network. The fracturing of the global economy has led to slower economic growth, increased protectionism, and disruptions to supply chains, but it can also give the United States some big advantages such as tariff revenue, reshoring of manufacturing and reduced trade deficits.

I think it is possible to grow the middle class, increase wages, and improve living standards or income for much of the middle class if the country can commit to production, not consumption, and use the elements of productivism to develop a comprehensive plan. It is perhaps the only chance for reversing the decline of the middle class and improving living standards for all workers.

CHAPTER 1

The Rise of Neoliberalism

Philosopher Isaiah Berlin summarized neoliberalism very succinctly when he said, "Freedom for the wolves has often meant death for the sheep."

In a 1970 article in *The New York Times*, Milton Friedman introduced a new doctrine which said "An entity's greatest responsibility lies in the satisfaction of the shareholders." In the 1990s, the Business Roundtable translated this into shareholder value or "the point of a business enterprise is to generate economic returns to its owners, period." And so, shareholder value and short-term profits became the driving force at the expense of employees, communities, the economy, and country.

Prior to his article, Milton Friedman and a man named Frederick Hayek had developed a new theory called neoliberalism, and along with globalization and free trade, these ideas suggested radical changes in the U.S. economy. Their theory was based on the assumption that free markets are the most efficient means of allocating resources with a minimum of state intervention and a commitment to the freedom of trade and capital. Neoliberalism was a 180-degree reversal from Keynesian economics used in the New Deal which was the first government program to give workers the right to organize, work safety and protection, union protection via the National Labor Relations Board (NLRB), and social security for retirement.

Neoliberalism is an ideology that emphasizes globalism, free trade, privatization, and deregulation. The idea emerged in the mid-twentieth century, and became a U.S. economic policy when multinational corporations (MNCs), with the support of the U.S. government, adopted globalism and began outsourcing to low-cost countries in the 1970s. It is not a program based on economic theory—it is political agenda based on free markets where there are definite winners and losers.

Things Began to Change

By 1970, America had 25 years of postwar growth, but the nation was facing rising global competition and corporate profits were being squeezed. The MNCs could have responded by improving product quality, protecting their technologies, and avoiding trade agreements that would sacrifice jobs, factories, communities, and manufacturing industries. But instead, they decided to reinvent their organizations and the new emphasis was on reducing costs, and achieving short-term profits.

Friedman argued in his 1970 article, all business decisions should be made to increase profits and with the financial interests of shareholders in mind first and foremost. Neoliberalism was supposed to reduce costs through privatization; deregulation; offshoring; and reduction in unions, wages, taxes, pensions, and government welfare programs. It also promoted the deregulation and acceptance of monopolies as indictors of greater efficiency. Milton Friedman's doctrine of shareholder value put neoliberalism into overdrive as a new business philosophy for American MNCs.

In essence, it meant rewriting the rules to advantage corporations, shareholders, and the wealthy, and to the disadvantage of labor and the average citizen. In fact, as the policy played out, the reality was social Darwinism for labor and free market capitalism for capital. Friedman and Hayek argued that the free-market economies were more efficient and delivered more economic freedoms and more prosperity. But they never said prosperity for who. In reality, it was freedom for some but not for others. The problem with most economic theories is that they always try to cover up or play down the problems of the losers. Philosopher Isaiah Berlin summarized neoliberalism very succinctly when he said, "Freedom for the wolves has often meant death for the sheep."

Neoliberalism was the theoretical foundation for radical economic changes and was closely connected to the strategy of outsourcing and globalization. It also began the slow hollowing of American industry.

One of the first strategies employed by the MNCs was to outsource production to low-wage countries. Outsourcing took the form of reliance on foreign suppliers to manufacture components or complete products, the introduction of coproduction arrangements (joint ventures), and licensing technology including technology transfer agreements.

Ronald Reagan

After being elected in 1980, Ronald Reagan openly embraced neoliberalism at every level of his administration including:

- **Union busting**—Reagan crushed the Traffic Controller's union which sent a signal to corporations that union busting was OK. Membership in private unions dropped from 35 percent in 1950 to 6 percent in 2023.

  1981: Economic Recovery and Tax Act—This bill was sold to the citizens as a recovery bill during the recession of 1981 to 83 that would create jobs. This was the beginning of what would become supply side economics. The bill reduced the highest rate of taxation from 70 to 50 percent overnight and vastly expanded corporate tax loopholes which lowered taxes for corporations by $150 billion over five years.

  1986: Tax Reform Act of 1986—A second tax Act was passed which was supposedly designed to simplify the tax code, broaden the tax base, and eliminate many tax shelters. Senator Portman (R-Ohio) called on Congress to pass comprehensive tax reform to boost the economy and ease the financial burden of families. The reality was the 1986 Tax Act lowered the top tax rate from 50 to 28 percent while the bottom rate was raised from 11 to 15 percent. The lower-class citizens were not represented in this Act and subsequently lost while the rich had a huge victory. As a result of the 1981 and 1986 bills, the top income tax rate was slashed from 70 to 28 percent.

- To pay for it, Reagan tripled the national debt from $800 billion in 1980 to $2.4 trillion in 1988. Suddenly, increasing the national debt was ok if it was for a good cause.

- He cut funding for public schools, but all religious, charter, and White private schools got federal dollars.

- He appointed Ray Donovan, a former construction executive and anti-labor partisan, as labor secretary.

- He supported monopolies and used the conservative judge Robert Bork to take a case to the supreme court changing the antitrust language to support monopolies by protecting consumers and efficiency, which pretty much ended Antitrust cases.

Neoliberalism also led to financial freedom and the unfettered growth of the financial sector. Reagan oversaw the deregulation of the financial industry which led to the collapse of the savings and loan banks during the Reagan administration requiring a government bailout of $100 billion. Financialization also put consumers on the hook by encouraging indebtedness and then trapping them by changing the rules of bankruptcies.

Neoliberalism had turned into Reaganomics. Reagan was a true supporter of the principles of Neoliberalism which changed how the government would approach the economy for the next 45 years.

Bill Clinton

When Bill Clinton decided to run for President, unions were declining and the Democratic Party could no longer count on the union political contributions. On the advice of his political consultants, Clinton decided to embrace corporate America and neoliberal ideology to make up for union money. He would not only embrace American corporations but would also enthusiastically embrace free trade. This would include Clinton and the Democratic Party:

- Abandoning unions and blue-collar workers in favor of the college elite.
- Embracing free trade, the service sector and importing, over domestic manufacturing and exporting.
- Promoting a reduction in welfare and the new line "the end of welfare as we know it."
- Taking a stand against big government in a 1996 speech when he said, "The era of big government is over."
- Embracing Wall Street and financialization when in 1999 he signed the Financial Services Modernization Act, which unraveled banking regulations and canceled the Glass–Steagall Act, which had outlawed the practice of Banks gambling with depositors' money.
- Support for the General Agreement on Tariffs and Trade (GATT) that kept US tariffs low and exports noncompetitive.

- The abandonment of American manufacturing and its workers with the signing of NAFTA and giving China most favored nation status.
- In 1996, Clinton signed the Telecommunications act which ended local ownership rules and allowed corporations to form monopolies by buying thousands of stations.

The support for free trade and globalism gutted the American middle class and was endorsed by all Democratic and Republican administrations after Reagan and Clinton.

George W. Bush

George W. Bush pushed through two huge tax reduction bills.

- **2001: Economic Growth and Tax Relief Reconciliation Act of 2001 (EGTRRA)**—Even though the country was sinking into a recession and deficits, it did not dissuade Republicans from pushing through more unbudgeted tax cuts. This tax cut was also sold to the citizens using supply side economics that promised jobs for tax breaks. In the fine print of the bill, was also included more itemized deductions for the wealthy as well as steep cuts in capital gains and dividend taxes. By employing "phase-ins" it appeared that the average citizen would get proportionate cuts for 10 years. But, instead, the average citizen would get a one-time $300 tax rebate and as the phased in tax cuts grew through the decade, the top 1 percent of tax payers received a 51 percent tax cut.
- **2003: Jobs and Growth Tax Relief and Reconciliation Act**—This bill was the second tax cut in the Bush Jr. administration and further lowered marginal tax rates—supposedly for all citizens. Since both the 2001 and 2003 bills were passed, the issue of who were the beneficiaries is still hotly debated. The Center on Budget and Policy Priorities concluded that "the largest benefits, accrue to the highest income households."[1] President George W. Bush's

---

[1] Joel Friedman and Isaac Shapiro, "Tax Returns: A Comprehensive Assessment of the Bush Administration's Record on Cutting Taxes," *CBBP*, July 1, 2010.

2001 cuts were followed by continued job losses for about a year because of the recession and it wasn't until after 2003 that jobs were created.

The tax cuts were neoliberal propaganda. The best analysis of the two Bush tax cuts was by the Center on Budget and Policy Priorities in 2008.[2] They found that the

1. Tax cuts didn't pay for themselves. Cutting taxes decreased revenues.
2. The economic expansion from 2001 to 2007 was subpar overall.
3. Extending the tax cuts without paying for them will reduce economic growth.
4. The tax cuts led to more inequality.
5. The tax cuts provided large gains for those with high incomes and little benefit to others.

George W. Bush also privatized health care when he successfully pushed through the Medicare Modernization Act of 2003 (MMA) which led to Medicare Advantage. Privatization did not save money, in fact, Medicare Advantage cost the federal government on average 11 percent more than conventional Medicare. In addition, the MMA did not include cost savings, and gave insurance companies the freedom to deny services to their customers.

Barack Obama

Instead of trying to end neoliberalism, President Obama continued to endorse free trade and globalism. He said "free trade seeks to promote growth, support more well-paying jobs in the United States, and strengthens the middle class." He also said "that trade policy done right—through proactive enforcement of existing agreements and the negotiation of new, high standard agreements—is among the nation's best tools to address the challenges of globalization and promote American interests and values."

---

[2]"Tax Cuts: Myths and Realities," *Center on Budget and Policy Priorities*, May 9, 2008.

He was also a supporter of the Trans Pacific Trade Agreement even though the evidence showed that trade agreements were killing manufacturing jobs and factories in the United States.

It is not clear whether Obama really believed in his free trade statement or that he knew there would be many losers but believed that free trade was still best for the majority.

In January of 2010, President Obama set an ambitious goal to double U.S. exports within five years, but he quickly ran into the problems of an overvalued dollar, outsourcing production, a rising trade deficit, and he backed away from the export goal and American manufacturing.

His Affordable Care Act (ACA), even though a blessing for millions of workers, also put the ACA into the hands of huge insurance companies thus extending the privatization of Medicare through Medicare Advantage

The adoption of neoliberalism and globalization by all Democratic and Republican Presidents since Reagan gutted the middle class, outsourced production and jobs, and crushed the hopes of workers and families in the deindustrialized cities and towns in the heartland. It was a god send for the wealthy and the shareholders of corporations, but has been very hard on average worker, particularly workers with a high school diploma or less.

Privatization of Public Services

The attempt to privatize public services like education, health care, and social security is fraught with problems. Public services were designed to support the majority of American citizens and changing the service to "for profit" is a contradiction of the original intent. The free market (privatization) approach has increased inequality in the provision of essential social services, resulting in long-term damage to the citizens, and cuts in the welfare state and public services.

Another experiment in privatization was during the Iraq war when thousands of jobs were taken from military service members and given to private contractors. The Commission on Wartime Contracting (CWC) estimated that the United States spent nearly $177 billion on private contractors in Iraq and Afghanistan by the end of 2010. Privatization of the military was not a profitable strategy in terms of neoliberal ideology or in terms of lower costs but it was very profitable for the large military contractors.

Neoliberalism has been criticized for promoting economic and political policies that help large corporations, such as government subsidies, tax breaks, and tax credits while cutting government money for unemployment, Social Security, Medicare and Medicaid. Strategies to reduce government costs will always be on the backs of the poor through cuts in the welfare state, and public services.

Conclusion

When capital has political power over the citizens it can lead to the erosion of democracy. Globalization and free trade weakened democratic nations like the United States by transferring trillions of dollars to China, Vietnam, and other Asian nations. The power of money in politics gives concentrated wealth a sword to hold over democracy's neck.

Neoliberalism, globalization, and free trade policies were the primary cause of the decline of the middle class. They were an almost religious commitment to economic policies that have shrunk the middle class, made the working class angry, sacrificed many industries, collapsed industrial capacity, reduced the number of skilled workers, and gave our foreign competitors our technologies.

The good news is that the era of neoliberalism, free trade, and globalism is coming to an end. The experiment was tried and has failed on many levels. It was a "scam to disempower the working class while enriching the already well off."

In his book *The Hidden History of Neoliberalism*, Thom Hartmann says,

> In overthrowing FDR's New Deal politics and economics, the Reagan's era destroyed most of the American labor movement, shifted trillions in both income and wealth from the middle class to the top 1%, consolidated business and the wealth it creates into the hands of monopolies in every sector of our economy, and moved over 60,000 factories and tens of millions of good paying jobs to low-wage countries, all while fattening the money bins of the morbidly rich with the Reagan, Bush, and Trump tax cuts.

CHAPTER 2

The Middle-Class Decline

The middle class has tried to use debt as a substitute for income to maintain a middle-class lifestyle, but in most instances, it is a losing proposition because they are not saving and are left living paycheck to paycheck.

The American middle class, once the foundation of the economy and the health of the nation, has been declining for decades. During this decline, our economic and political leaders raved about the exceptional performance of the economy in terms of the rising stock market, low unemployment rate, and the new jobs created. George W. Bush's council of economic advisers summed up the excellent performance by saying "The U.S. economy is on solid footing for sustained growth in the years ahead." But the reality was that many in the middle class were hurting and had been hurting since 1980. Despite all of the talk about prosperity much of the middle class was in decline.

According to a Pew Research Center analysis of government data, the middle class, has steadily contracted in the past five decades. The share of adults who live in middle-class households fell from 61 percent in 1971 to 50 percent in 2021 (Figure 2.1).

Another example of the decline is Figure 2.2, which shows the decline of middle-class share of national income since 1967. This 7 percent loss is equal to $3 trillion of lost income.

For decades following the end of World War II, inflation-adjusted hourly compensation (including employer-provided benefits as well as

Figure 2.1 The declining middle class

Source: Pew Research Center, How the American middle class has changed in the past five decades, April 20, 2022.

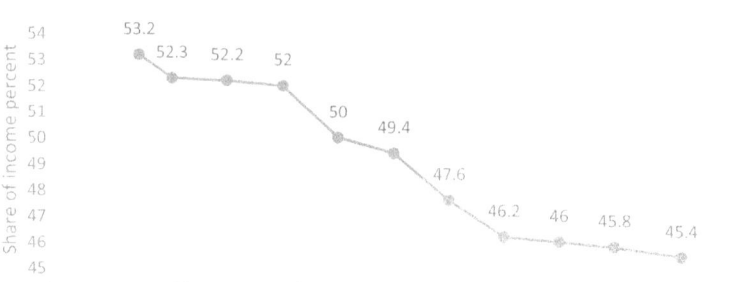

Figure 2.2 Middle-class share of national income (1967 to 2016)

Source: Bureau of the Census, Table H-2. Share of Aggregate Income Received by Each Fifth and Top 5 Percent of Households (U.S. Department of Commerce), available at https://www.census.gov/data/tables/time-series/demo/income-poverty/historical-income-households.html (last accessed September 2017).

wages) for the vast majority of American workers rose in line with increases in economywide productivity. Thus, hourly pay became the primary mechanism that transmitted an increase in living standards.

Since 1973, hourly compensation of the vast majority of American workers has not risen in line with economywide productivity. Net productivity grew 80.9 percent between 1979 and 2024. Yet inflation-adjusted hourly compensation of the median worker rose just 29.4 percent, over this same period. Productivity has grown 2.7× as much as pay, which left wages for most workers flat. In keeping with the commitment to short term profits and shareholder value, instead, the money that could have gone to wages went to executive compensation, shareholders, and company profits.

These trends began in the early 1980s, when corporations looked for ways to reduce labor costs. There was growing use of temporary workers, part-time workers, two tier pay systems, the rise of contract workers and the gig economy, which includes all non-full-time jobs. The massive downsizing of the permanent workforce was spectacularly successful.

Wage suppression was generated by policy choices that resulted in excessive unemployment, eroded unionization, stagnant wages, and imposed noncompete contract clauses, to the benefit of large firms.

Figure 2.3 shows the cumulative change in real annual wages, by wage group, from 1979 to 2019. The top 1 percent of earners, experienced a

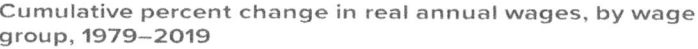

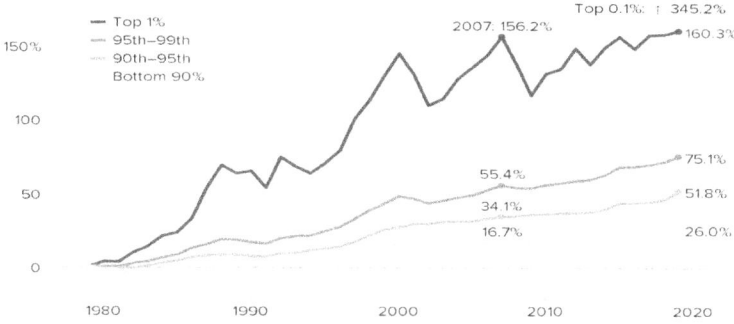

Figure 2.3 Changes in wages by income group (1979 to 2019)

Source: EPI analysis of Kopczuk, Saez, and Song (2007, Table A3) and Social Security Administration wage statistics, Economic Policy Institute.

160.3 percent increase in wages, while the bottom 90 percent grew by only 26.0 percent over the 40-year period The top 0.1 percent: saw even faster growth, with wages increasing by 345.2 percent. This long-term trend led to serious inequality that was driven by factors like:

- Workers with higher education levels saw much faster wage growth than those with less education, contributing to a widening wage gap.
- A general decline in the ability of workers to negotiate for higher wages as union membership declined (Figure 2.5).
- Five tax laws that reduced the taxes of the wealthy.

These three economic factors contributed to inequality and the widening wage gap between the top and bottom earners.

Figure 2.4 illustrates the growing gap between upper income and middle and lower households since 1970 that drove the rise in income inequality. The decline was not the result of a single cause but a confluence of policies including: the shift to globalization and free trade, and the adoption of neoliberalism philosophies by both the government and corporations. These policies led to the rise in income inequality. It was a one-sided economic change that rewarded capital at the expense of labor.

The gaps in income between upper-income and middle- and lower-income households are rising, and the share held by middle-income households is falling

Median household income, in 2018 dollars, and share of U.S. aggregate household income, by income tier

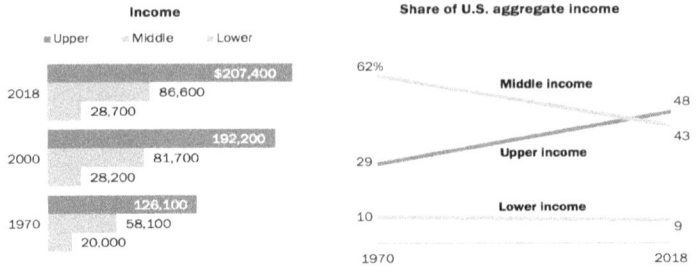

Note: Households are assigned to income tiers based on their size-adjusted income. Incomes are scaled to reflect a three person household. Revisions to the Current Population Survey affect the comparison of income data from 2014 onwards. See Methodology for details.

Figure 2.4 Income gaps and the rise in inequality

Source: Pew Research Center analysis of the Current Population Survey, Annual Social and Economic Supplements (IPUMS). "Most Americans Say There Is Too Much Economic Inequality in the U.S., but Fewer Than Half Call It a Top Priority.

Since 1980, there have been some astounding shocks to the middle class. It was a period George Packer calls the unwinding

The following are the most important factors that led to the decline:

1. **Automation**: The blue-collar jobs that many of my friends found after high school have been mostly eliminated by automation. I was in the automation business for many years, manufacturing palletizers and robots for production lines that would eliminate at least one person per shift. So today, the low-skilled jobs for the high school graduate are a rarity, and the new problem for manufacturing is to find highly skilled workers to maintain and troubleshoot all of this automation equipment.

2. **Job Losses:** During the period of deindustrialization, beginning in 1980, American manufacturing lost 7.5 million jobs mostly to outsourcing and automation. For every person directly employed in manufacturing, manufacturing output supports more than 2.3 jobs elsewhere in the economy, which means the total loss was 17.5 million jobs.

   The big problem for laid-off workers with a high school diploma was that most had to take service industry jobs that were a serious reduction in wage and benefits.

3. **Outsourcing**: The beginning of outsourcing was coincident with the move toward short-term profits and shareholder value, and the deindustrialization of America. According to the Economic Policy Institute, American corporations have outsourced more than 5 million jobs and 91,000 plants since 1997.[1] When it is easy to procure cheap imported goods, there is less pressure to raise domestic wages, and, in fact, there is pressure to reduce wages.

4. **RTM:** This is a statistical phenomenon describing how variables much higher or lower than the mean are often much closer to the mean when measured a second time. Outsourcing caused RTM which pitted American workers against low wage workers around the world. If foreign wages are $3 per hour and American wages are $20 per hour, the pressure from the mean puts pressure on the wages of the high wage country which over time reduces American wages closer to the mean of foreign wages. RTM was a disaster for the American middle class, and led to wage stagnation and reduction.

   The paper "On the Persistence of the China Shock,"[2] by David Autor, David Dorn, and Gordon Hanson, says that of 722 U.S. regions analyzed, 223 of them, or 32.8 percent, suffered absolute declines in real per capita income. This means that "the open door for Chinese imports reduced the incomes of one third of the U.S. public."[3] They go on to say that "Trade with China is effectively a vehicle to transfer income from working class in the heartland to the affluent, who live mostly on both coasts." Giving China the most favored nation status became the final nail in the coffin for American blue-collar manufacturing workers.

5. **Trade agreements**: It was the 1993 fight over the North American Free Trade Agreement that saw the Clinton wing of the Democratic Party stick the knife into the back of its longtime ally—organized labor. President Bill Clinton surrounded himself with Wall Street financiers who blamed stagnant wages on the workers themselves

---

[1] Robert E. Scott, August 10, 2020, Trump's trade policies have cost thousands of U.S. manufacturing jobs, Economic Policy Institute.
[2] David Autor, David Dorn, and Gordon Hanson, "On the Persistence of the China Shock," NBER Working Paper 29401, October 2021, page 1.
[3] *Ibid.*

and their lack of skills and education, and unwillingness to relocate. The NAFTA betrayal, plus the many free trade deals that followed, rankled union members for years. In fact, the head of the Teamsters Union would not endorse Kamala Harris during the 2024 election because of NAFTA, and many United Auto Workers did not vote for Democrats in Wisconsin, Michigan, and Pennsylvania.

6. **The decline of unions:** The United States Bureau of Labor Statistics recently reported that the nation's unionization rate—the proportion of employed workers who are union members—is now the lowest on record, at 10 percent for public and private unions. Only one in 10 American workers is a union member, down from nearly one in three workers during the 1950s.

   In 1981, the Reagan administration helped corporations by terminating the air traffic control employees and crushing their union, which began a lengthy period of union busting by the big corporations. The following chart shows what happened to both the middle-class wages and unions since the 1960s. At the same time middle class share of aggregate income declined from 53 percent in 1967 to 45 percent in 2014 (see Figure 2.2). A rising share of the nation's income was going to capital and a declining share to labor.

   Unions played a crucial role in raising pay, benefits, and workplace standards, and their decline over this period reduced workers' bargaining power and contributed to wage stagnation for middle-income earners. Collective bargaining through unions had allowed workers to earn 15 to 20 percent more than people in nonunion jobs. The erosion of collective bargaining has been a key factor in the decline of household income for the middle class (Figure 2.5).

7. **Debt and Easy Credit:** In the late 1970s, when wages began to stagnate the middle class tried to keep up their buying power by women going to work, working longer hours, drawing down savings, and going into debt. As financial regulations slowly collapsed along with oversight of consumer and mortgage lending, Wall Street introduced predatory lending in the form of high-interest rate credit cards with fees and penalties, payday loans, and

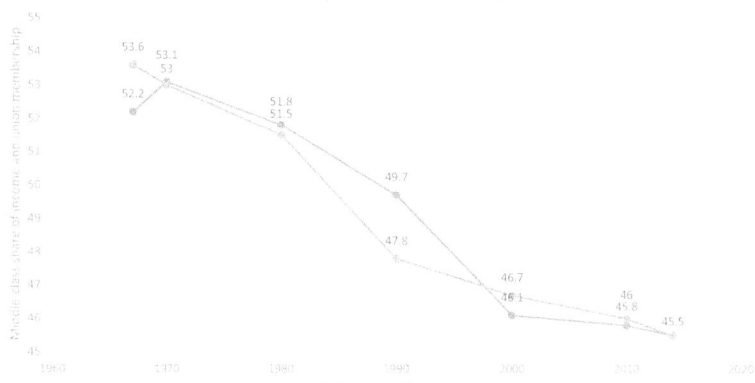

Figure 2.5 Union membership in the United States (1930 to 2010) and middle-class income

Source: Union membership in the U.S., 1930–2010 and middle class income, Monthly Labor Review, The Census Bureau, 2015.

subprime mortgages. The predatory lending practices "preyed on the middle class and made them poorer."

In 1970 about 50 percent of U.S. families had credit cards. By 2001, the usage jumped to 75 percent. There is no problem if the user pays off his debt every month. But users who carry debt from month to month, called revolvers, accumulate interest and fees. According to the Federal Reserve, the average credit card interest rate on accounts with balances assessed interest was 22.80 percent in November 2024. Experian reports that as of 2023, the average U.S. consumer owed $6,501 on their credit cards and the delinquency rate was 13.4 percent in the United States.[4] According to data released by the Federal Reserve, credit card balances reached $1.21 trillion at the end of December 2024.[5] This figure represents a meaningful increase compared to the country's prepandemic credit card debt high of $927 billion. Interest and fees from credit cards have put many

---

[4]Mike Rogoway, August 24, 2925, Oregon credit a card debt jumped 25% in three years, The Oregonian.
[5]"Household Debt Balances Continue Steady Increase; Delinquency Transition Rates Remain Elevated for Auto and Credit Cards," *Federal Reserve Bank of New York*, February 13, 2025.

middle-class families into a position where they cannot get ahead. They are like heroin addicts who see the solution as more heroin.

Since 1980, student loan debt has increased significantly, with the total amount owed by Americans soaring from $24 billion in 1990 to 1991 to over $1.6 trillion by 2024, which is 42 percent more than a decade earlier. The aggregate volume of new student borrowing has increased more than fourfold over the past 20 years.

The middle class has *tried to use debt as a substitute for income* to maintain a middle-class lifestyle, but in most instances, it is a losing proposition because they are not saving and are left living paycheck to paycheck.

8. **Deregulation of the financial industry:** The deregulation of the financial industry, particularly during the 1980s and 1990s, contributed to increased economic inequality, which led to a wave of risky financial activities that culminated in the 2008 (subprime) financial crisis. Middle-class Americans bore the brunt of this crisis through job losses, home foreclosures, and reduced savings. The 2008 financial crisis resulted in a loss of approximately $15.4 trillion in household wealth disproportionately affecting middle-class families.[6] The crisis was precipitated by the collapse of the housing market, driven by speculative and predatory lending practices. When the bubble burst, millions of middle-class Americans found themselves underwater on their mortgages, leading to a cascade of foreclosures and financial ruin.

9. **Rising prices:** Essential costs like health care, education, and housing have skyrocketed, squeezing the middle class and reducing living standards.

The median price of a new home in 1980 was around $68,000, while the median price today is about $426,000. In 1980, per-person annual spending on health care was $932. By 2022, this increased to $11,193. Tuition and fees at four-year institutions were $5,000 a year in 1980 to 1981 and $17,250 a year in 2021 to 2022.

If you can't buy a home and have to rent it is also a problem. Since 1980, the average rent for a two-bedroom apartment has increased significantly, with the median monthly rent in 1980 being

---

[6]Benjamin Landy, "A Tale of Two Recoveries: Wealth Inequality After the Great Recession," *The Century Foundation*, August 28, 2013.

around $243 and rising to an average of $1,388 in August 2022. This represents an average annual increase of almost 9 percent. In addition, there are very few low-cost rentals available which has led to hundreds of thousands of homeless men, women, and children who live on the streets or in shelters in most major cities.

Today, millions of middle-class citizens cannot buy a home, afford health care or afford to go to college. They have been consumed by inflation and are angry and worried about their future as was evident in the 2024 election.

10. **Bankruptcies***:* In 1980 the filing rate for bankruptcies was 1.3 per 1000 people. By 2024 the filing rate was 5.3 per 1000 people, more than four times the 1980 rate, and 80 times the 1920 rate. The primary reasons were the increase in consumer debt, decreased savings, and the low costs to file. As the middle class was squeezed between wage stagnation and the rising cost of living, more people could not handle income shocks like divorce, job loss, death of a spouse, or major medical expenses. The big banks did not like the growing bankruptcy rate and lobbied Congress who passed the Bankruptcy Abuse and Consumer Protection Act of 2005 designed to decrease the growth of bankruptcies. The very corporations who designed the easy credit schemes now wanted to punish the users.

11. **Poverty Rate:** In 2023 the official government poverty rate in the United States was 38.6 million people. If you lose your job in European countries the Safety nets include income assistance, universal health care, and a universal pension system. The United States has the least generous safety net system of all Western Countries.

Globalization and the rise of neoliberalism as a political ideology turned out to be a trap where the average middle-class citizen bore the brunt of the economic crisis through job losses, stagnant wages, and not being able to keep up with inflation. Not since the Gilded Age have the wealthy accumulated so much wealth leading to so much inequality and misery for much of the middle class.

The costs of buying a home, paying for college, buying a car, obtaining health care, affording day care, and retiring have become problematic. For many in the middle class it has become a race to the bottom.

CHAPTER 3

Winners and Losers of the Free Market

It is time to face the fact that America turned its back on communities in the heartland and workers in support of free trade and cheap imports.

All presidents, from Reagan to Biden, Republican and Democrat, supported free trade and globalization. The problem with economic theories like free trade is that they always cover up or down play what happens to the losers. They knew there would be losers in free trade but believed that the benefits outweighed the downside. But for millions of workers, free trade meant shifting them into low-wage jobs and the slide into economic oblivion. Globalization and free trade became a one-sided process where the benefits would flow to capital and the costs to labor.

Worker Insecurity

Perhaps the most common criticism of neoliberalism and globalization is that their policies have led to class-based economic inequality, while allowing—if not exacerbating—poverty. There is a new class of people forced to live precariously without any predictability or security. These are middle-class and lower-class workers who are angry and frustrated, and worried about their futures.

When the philosophy of neoliberalism became the philosophy of the government it led to a lack of concern for actual well-being of the losers. For those left behind in the new system, there is a feeling of powerlessness. The primary problem is that the system now supports the minority with no regard for the majority. The criticism that, in prioritizing privatization and giving tax cuts to corporations and the wealthy, neoliberalism disincentivizes practices that would improve the human condition and imposed austerity for everyone else.

Millions of households are living paycheck to paycheck in the sense that their necessity spending is close to their total household income. The definition is that household necessity spending exceeds 95 percent of their household income.

Abandonment of Cities and Towns in the Heartland

As outsourcing progressed since 1980, millions of workers lost their jobs and cities and towns in the heartland were economically destroyed. The sudden loss of manufacturing jobs created an economic "ripple effect," where people move away, the tax base is reduced, which in turn leads to cuts in public services like police and fire protection; the closing of small retail shops, grocery stores, and the boarding up of businesses; the foreclosure and abandonment of homes; and falling home prices. Contrary to the optimistic predictions by economists, the transition to the service economy has not generated good jobs for people who lost manufacturing jobs. Most were forced to take lower-pay and lower-hour service jobs.

The United States did not have the social programs or safety net to help these communities, and ignoring the people who were facing new economic problems has led to the rise of populism, general unrest, and a divided country. We now face long-term changes in the economy where millions struggle. If globalism and free trade are good for the nation, as proposed by economists, why haven't the benefits reached all of these towns and cities? The answer is that these workers and cities were sacrificed so that consumers could enjoy cheap imported goods and the rich could get richer. It is time to face the fact that America turned its back on these communities and workers in support of free trade and cheap imports.

Deaths of Despair

The book *Deaths of Despair* by Anne Case and Angus Deaton describes "life on the edge" for hundreds of thousands of blue-collar workers. They make the argument that globalism and the decline of manufacturing have led to a surge in deaths of despair from suicide, drug overdose, and alcoholism, claiming hundreds of thousands of American lives. As the college educated became healthier and wealthier, adults without a degree are literally dying from pain and despair. The authors make the case that "the weakening position of labor, the growing power of corporations and rapacious healthcare sector redistributes working-class wages into the pockets of the wealthy."[1]

Winners and Losers

In neoliberalism, inequality is acceptable because the market rewards winners and punishes those who are not able to carry their own weight (losers). The big problem for the losers was that wages did not keep up with living costs and millions of people fell behind.

Robert Reich in his article "The Myth of the Free Market" observes:

> If some people aren't paid enough to live on, the market has determined they aren't worth enough. If others rake in billions, they must be worth it. If millions of Americans remain unemployed or their paychecks are shrinking, or they work two or three part-time jobs with no idea what they will earn next month or next week, that's too bad; it's just the outcome of the market.[2]

This sad statement is what happened to millions of workers.

The book *The Hidden History of Neoliberalism*, by Thom Hartmann, describes losers in terms of inequality. He says, "Inequality is a sign that society is working as it should because the market rewards the most competent and punishes or leaves behind those not able or willing to carry their own weight." This statement was prophetic because it was an accurate statement of what happened to the losers in the middle class.

Everyone knows there are winners and losers when capitalism is functioning at its best. Capitalist hardliners say that "the winners are those who are honest, industrious, thoughtful, prudent, frugal, responsible,

---

[1]Anne Case and Angus Deaton, *Deaths of Despair and the Future of Capitalism* (Princeton University Press, 2020).
[2]Robert Reich, September 16, 2013, The Myth of the "Free Market" and How to Make the Economy Work for Us.

disciplined and efficient. The losers are those who are shiftless, lazy, imprudent, extravagant, negligent, impractical and inefficient." This is followed by the assumption that capitalism rewards winners and punishes losers.

This is absolutist thinking that doesn't acknowledge that many of these losers are defenseless children, retired people, people with disabilities, and people who work hard and are struggling from paycheck to paycheck in low-wage jobs. Of course, there will be laggards and abusers but many of these people (losers) are the most vulnerable citizens in the society who have no alternatives.

In neoliberalism only the strong and worthy survive in society and the new economy. It is social Darwinism for people without the skills or education to compete in the new society, and the losers get what they deserve.

The Failure of the Service Economy

Many economists and academics jumped on the "postindustrial" bandwagon and have tried to convince most citizens that the transition to the postindustrial service economy is a good thing. Michael Boskin, who was economic adviser to George H. Bush said, "It doesn't make any difference whether a country makes computer chips or potato chips." His flippant remark is incorrect, and as it turns out, not only was making chips important for the United States, but the shortage of U.S. made chips (microprocessors) reduced automobile production, and required a federal bailout of the semiconductor industry to the tune of $52 billion in taxpayer dollars.

Larry Summers, former economics adviser to President Obama is also a proponent of the transition to a service economy. He, like most economists, believes in the importance of importing low-priced goods, and believes that it is a substantial part of what determines the living standards of Americans.

The Peterson Institute for International Economics estimated some time ago that free trade, reduced costs for consumers by more than a $trillion dollars and that if we had removed our tariffs and other measures, it would've added 2 percent to people's real incomes by reducing inflation pressure.

Many economists believed that the service economy and cheap imported goods would provide economic growth, good jobs and improved living standards for the middle class. But it just didn't happen for the majority of the middle class. The price of cheap imported goods was not enough to offset the stagnant wages and rising living costs of most workers.

Supporters of globalization and the postindustrial service economy believed that free trade, and market forces would shift the workforce to "more productive uses, allowing more efficient industries to thrive" and bringing higher wages, job creation, and a more vibrant economy overall. Let's examine these assumptions:

> **Shift the workforce to "more productive uses:** A monthly Index called the Job Quality Index (JQI) shows a very different view of the workforce than the economist view that we can just "shift the workforce to more productive uses." The Job Quality Index measures higher wage/higher hour jobs versus lower wage/lower hour jobs. The index chart below shows that since 1990, job quality as measured by the income earned by workers, has significantly declined. Less hours worked with less pay and little room for growth is becoming the norm.
>
> **Job creation:** Manufacturing has lost about 7.5 million employees since 1979, and private service-providing industries accounted for more than 90 percent of the net employment gain from 1979 to 2001. Figure 3.1 shows that the economy has produced a lot of jobs but they are increasingly "low quality" service jobs. The JQI chart shows that the quality of new jobs has been decreasing for 30 years.
>
> **Allowing more efficient industries to thrive:** According to the Bureau of Labor Statistics for the period of 2001 to 2024, 36 out of 38 NAISC manufacturing industries continued to lose factories and employees. One of the service industries with the most growth is Leisure and Hospitality: Employment in this sector has seen robust growth since 1990, with food services and drinking places being a major driver. But the industry is mostly composed of low-quality jobs.

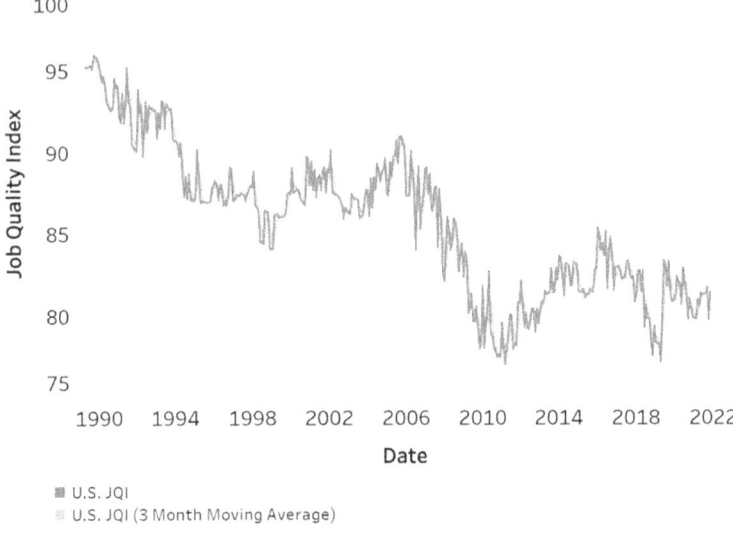

The U.S. Private Sector Job Quality Index

Figure 3.1 Job quality index (1990 to 2022)

A more vibrant economy: The smooth transition to the service economy has become a very rough road, creating many losers, angry, and frustrated voters. The price of cheap imported goods was not enough to offset the stagnant wages of most workers. It has not been a vibrant economy for millions of workers.

The American social contract, "a promise of opportunity and security for those who act responsibly," is fundamentally broken. For working Americans, particularly workers with a high school diploma, it became a race to the bottom.

CHAPTER 4

The Decline of Manufacturing

The decline of manufacturing is the high price we pay for cheap imports.

At the end of World War II, America emerged with 50 percent share of all manufactured goods sold in the world economy. Since the United States was in a dominant position, they chose to ignore tariffs, value-added taxes, and trade barriers, from most other countries. The U.S. government then became a champion of Free Trade with no or low tariffs.

From 1940 to 1980 the middle class enjoyed rising living standards and wages. But after 1980, wages became stagnant, the cost of living exceeded wages, trade deficits expanded exponentially, and foreign competitors began taking over our industries and technologies. Looking at where we are today in terms of unfair free trade, the decline of manufacturing, and the decline of the middle class; I wonder how it all went wrong.

The Decline of American Manufacturing

Figure 4.1 shows that manufacturing employment in the United States has hit its lowest share of the U.S. workforce since modern records began in 1939. At 8.3 percent in June 2025, American manufacturing employment is at an all-time low. We are far from the days of the 1950s and 1960s when manufacturing made up more than 30 percent of the workforce, the U.S. economy grew by 2 to 4 percent a year, and family incomes rose steadily. Manufacturing has also traditionally been a route to a middle-class lifestyle for those without a four-year college degree. And 65 percent of U.S. workers do not have a four-year degree.

The following chart from the CPA and the world bank shows that most of our foreign competitors have a manufacturing gross domestic product (GDP) between 13 and 25 percent. "U.S. manufacturing has

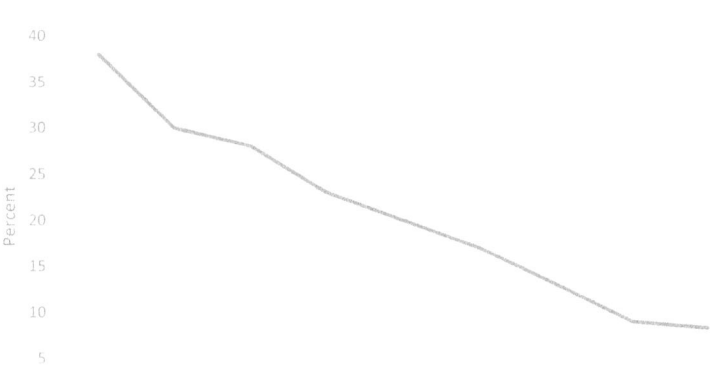

Figure 4.1 Percent of the workforce in manufacturing

Source: Coalition for Prosperous America. 3 charts approved by Nick Iacovella on October 21, 2025. Manufacturing Employment Hits All-Time Low. Will IRA Reverse the Trend? Coalition for a Prosperous America.

fallen from 21 to 25 percent of Gross Domestic Product, in the 1950s to about 10 percent today. The result is an unbalanced economy excessively dominated by services and imports."

CPA argues that "lack of economic diversity, and the resulting concentration in services, and the financial sector, makes the US more fragile and less resilient in times of peace as well as in times of crisis." (Figure 4.2)

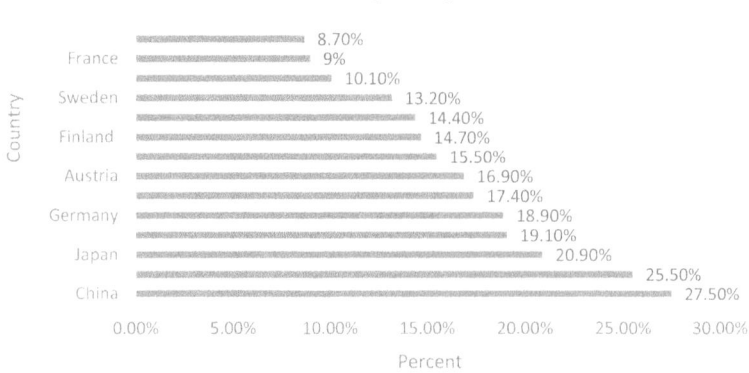

Figure 4.2 Manufacturing as a percent of GDP

Source: World Bank.

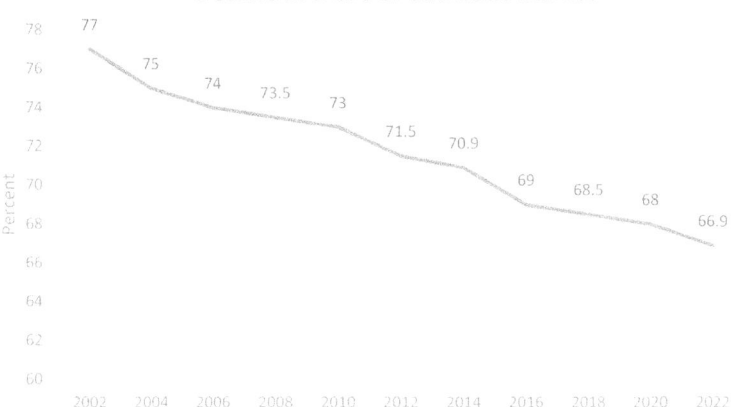

Figure 4.3 Decline in share of domestic market

Source: U.S. Bureau of Economic Analysis, U.S. Census; CPA Calculations (Annual Figures).

Decline in Share of Domestic Market

The above chart (Figure 4.3) also reveals the seriousness of American Manufacturing's decline. All of our foreign competitors have access to our market, the biggest consumer market in the world, while American manufacturers have lost 11 percent of our domestic market since China was given most favored nation status in 2002. A Domestic Market Share Index of 66.9 percent means that foreign producers hold about one-third of the U.S. market for manufactured goods in the form of imports.

In my travels I have found that few citizens understand how or why the United States lost so much of our domestic manufacturing sector. The decline of manufacturing is the high price we pay for cheap imports. We need a new industrial policy that grows manufacturing back to 15 percent of GDP, and the Trump administration needs to do more than just implement tariffs—they need to set a specific goal for the percent of GDP they want to attain.

Table 4.1 is a comparison of manufacturing weekly wages in 2023 to the Leisure/Hospitality and the social assistance industries, where many people who have lost their jobs in manufacturing end up. The average weekly earnings are not sufficient to maintain their previous living standards and the worker usually doesn't get a full 40-hour work week.

Table 4.1 Manufacturing pays higher weekly wages than other sectors

Sector	NAICS sector code	Total employment (millions)	Average hourly wage	Average weekly earnings	Earnings discount to mfg. earnings
Manufacturing	31, 32, 33	12.99	$32.38	$1,298.44	100
Leisure/ Hospitality	71,72	16.58	$21.21	$538.73	−58.5%
Health Care/Social Assistance	62	21.35	$33.14	$1,106.88	−14.8%

Source: Bureau of Labor Statistics. All data for June 2023.

Workers with a high school diploma or less who transition to the service industries, are more than likely to see a reduction in income and benefits.

Why Economists Don't Believe Manufacturing Is Vital to the Economy?

Many economists and academics jumped on the "postindustrial service" bandwagon and have tried to convince citizens that the transition is a good and inevitable thing. Christine Romer, who was chairwoman of Obama's Council of Economic Advisers, thinks that the service economy is as important as manufacturing and haircuts are just as important as hairdryers. She believes her views are representative of orthodox economic wisdom. She said, "Everyone laments the decline of American manufacturing, but there's no good reason to give that sector of the economy special government support."

Larry Summers, the former director of President Obama's National Economic Council said, "America's role is to feed the global economy that's increasingly based on knowledge and services rather than making stuff." Summers also says, "It is wrong to suppose that manufacturing-based economic nationalism is a route to higher incomes or better standards of living for the middle class."

The big question is, Can the United States' transition to a service economy still provide enough good jobs and a standard of living for most of the middle class? Neither Christine Romer or Larry Summers can answer this question, but the fact that the majority of the middle class is unhappy with their living standards seems to negate Summers and Romer's arguments.

If you are among the 65 percent of workers who have a high school diploma or less, you are probably struggling to make ends meet and the service economy has not provided an answer. As the recent election proved, millions of workers in this category feel that something is very wrong in the postindustrial service economy and are angry and worried about their future.

The second question that they don't explain is how a service economy can replace manufacturing and produce the kind of economic growth and innovation we had prior to 1980.

Alexander Hamilton said that real wealth doesn't exist until somebody makes something. I believe he is correct, and contrary to what Romer and Summers believe, the service economy is an oxymoron.

The best summary of the fallacy of the postindustrial service economy was summarized by Harold Myerson in *The Washington Post*. He said, "The Wall Street/Wal-Mart economy of the past several decades offshored millions of factory jobs, which it offset by creating low-paying jobs in the service and retail sectors: extending credit to consumers so they could keep consuming despite their stagnating incomes; and fueling, until it collapsed, a boom in construction." He also writes that

> of all the lies that the American people have been told in the past four decades, the biggest one may be this: **We'll all come out ahead in the shift from an industrial to post-industrial society.** The post-industrial economy turned out to be a bust. The time for neo-industrial America has arrived.

Free Trade Agreements

For 30 years free trade and trade agreements were considered a good thing where most citizens would benefit. Doubters were considered radicals who didn't understand the natural transition to the postindustrial service economy. Barack Obama said, "While some communities have suffered from foreign competition, trade has helped our economy much more than it has hurt." But after NAFTA and giving China most favored nation status, most citizens know that the politicians and economists were wrong, and free trade has hurt working people and manufacturing a lot more than it helped.

Free Trade has become a class issue where working people absorbed the losses and the owners (capital) pocketed the benefits. Today we now know that since year 2000, America lost 4.0 million jobs as a result of deindustrialization and free trade.

Granting China Most Favored Nation Status MFN

On October 10, 2000, President Bill Clinton signed into law a historic bill granting Permanent Normal Trade Relations (PNTR) to China with the *hope* that China would become more democratic. China has ignored the agreement and exploited the United States using predatory mercantilism, while our government chose to ignore China's cheating and not enforce the rules of the agreement. As investment in plants in China and Asia grew, multinational corporations (MNCs) accelerated outsourcing of jobs and production to China, and our trade deficit began to grow. The Growth in America's trade deficit with China since 2001 has resulted in the loss of nearly 4 million domestic jobs—a quarter of which were in California and Texas—according to a report from the Economic Policy Institute.[1]

There is nothing moral, or even inevitable about the history of globalization and free trade. From the point of view of most of the middle class it was part of the Globalization trap.

Outsourcing

In the 1970s, American corporations were confronted with serious international economic competition. The profits that the corporations had enjoyed since the beginning of World War II began to erode. This began an era of "corporate restructuring." Their primary strategy was to outsource their production to low-cost countries. So began the rise of

---

[1]Andrew Soergel, January 30, 2020, California and Texas among biggest losers of jobs from growing China Trade deficit, U.S. News.

trade deficits and imports and the decline of exports and jobs. Outsourcing took the form of reliance on foreign suppliers, the introduction of joint venture agreements, and licensing technology including technology transfer agreements. It also began the move toward short-term profits and shareholder value and the slow hollowing of American industry known as deindustrialization.

Academics and most economists supported outsourcing because they believed it would provide cheap products to consumers and that America could transition to a service economy that would provide good jobs and living standards to the middle class. However, 40 years of outsourcing to low-cost countries pushed the trade deficit to $1.3 trillion in 2024. The Blue-Collar Institute believes that $1 trillion in goods trade deficit equals 5.7 million jobs lost.

Manufacturing jobs are not the same as other jobs in the economy. Manufacturing jobs pay more and are a source of good jobs for workers with a high school diploma or less. The loss of one manufacturing job means the loss of 2.3 other jobs in the economy. Outsourcing also, gave our trade competitors our products and technologies. Outsourcing and free trade agreements have bled America dry.

According to the CPA, the China trade deficit alone cost the United States 3.82 million jobs, including 2.82 million manufacturing jobs. An example of what happened as result of NAFTA and outsourcing is the U.S. textile industry. In 1993, Dan River Mills in Danville Virginia had 6,500 employees operating seven mills. But, after Congress approved NAFTA in 1995, Dan River began laying off their employees and by 2001 they were all gone.

In Bruceton Tennessee, the Henry I. Siegel company (HIS), manufactured jeans and suits in three large textile plants employing 1,700 workers. After NAFTA HIS went into free fall and the last 55 employees were laid off in 2000. In fact, according to the Bureau of Labor Statistics, since 2002, 197,449 textile manufacturing jobs have been lost, and 2,877 textile plants in the United States were closed.

What began as a trickle of textile products turned into an avalanche of outsourcing in line with the multinational corporate goals of short-term profits and increasing shareholder value. In addition, 292,752 furniture jobs and 5695 machinist jobs were lost during this same period.

The Democratic Party Coalition

From 1930 to 1980, the Democratic Party had a coalition that included minorities, farmworkers, women, blue-collar and union workers that represented labor. But in 1993, President Bill Clinton helped pass the North American Free Trade Agreement. Clinton publicly promised that NAFTA would increase the existing trade surplus, creating 200,000 new American jobs in its first two years, and a million jobs in five years. But a report from the Economic Policy Institute proved that between 1993 and 2013 the trade deficits caused by NAFTA displaced 851,700 U.S. jobs.

The Democratic Party under Clinton had sold out blue-collar workers and had stabbed the unions in the back. The party abandoned blue-collar workers in favor of college-educated workers, and many blue-collar and union workers supported Trump in 2024 election. Now the Democratic Party is scrambling to find new voters but they are going to have to prove that they are supportive of manufacturing, blue-collar workers, and the people in the middle class who are struggling paycheck to paycheck, if they want a new coalition.

I have been following manufacturing industries for many years (2002 to 2024), in terms of the changes in employment and establishments. The data in Table 4.2 show the inconvenient truth—that 36 of 38 manufacturing industries continue to decline in terms of both number of plants and employees.

Some of the industries, such as textiles, apparel, furniture, hardware, cutlery, and hand tools have been declining for many decades and are probably beyond recovery because they have lost their markets to foreign competitors.

But the most perplexing of these declining industries are the ones that are fundamental to making other manufactured products. These are industries like machining, machine tools, mold making, tool and die, semiconductors, forging, and foundries. It is difficult to see how we can ever achieve a manufacturing renaissance, or maintain an industrial sector, while these critical industries continue to decline.

Table 4.2 NAISC Industry data on establishments and employment

NAISC Code	Industry	2002 Establish	2002 Employ	2023 Establish	2023 Employ	Changes since 2002 Establish	%	Employ	%
3132	Textile fabric mills	1,935	145,214	1,091	43,265	-844	-44	-101,949	-70
3141	Textile furnishings	3,261	116,429	1,575	40,243	-1,686	-52	-76,186	-65
3149	Other textile mills	5,141	77,956	4,794	58,685	-347	-7	-19,271	-25
31521	Cut and sew apparel	6,814	112,416	2,327	21,684	-4,487	-66	-90,732	-81
321911	Wood doors and windows	1,482	71,674	1,209	57,842	-273	-18	-13,832	-19
321918	Other millwork and floors	2,606	60,044	1,722	33,305	-884	-34	-26,739	-45
321920	Wood containers/pallets	3,549	60,371	3,172	64,339	-377	-11	-3,968	-7
322121	Paper (except newsprint)	637	106,423	512	49,767	-125	-20	-56,656	-53
322130	Paperboard mills	296	40,349	275	31,964	-21	-7	-8,385	-21
322211	Corrugated box manufacturing	1,983	127,526	1,631	102,864	-352	-18	-24,662	-19
326121	Unlaminated plastics	656	30,038	476	22,642	-180	-27	-7,396	-25
326122	Plastic pipe and fittings	669	30,960	639	32,279	-30	-4	1,319	4
326211	Tires except retreading	168	66,375	187	52,148	19	11	-14,227	-21
326291	Rubber for mechanical use	626	48,505	483	28,176	-143	-23	-20,329	-42
326299	All other rubber products	758	31,744	706	24,308	-52	-7	-7,436	-23
327110	Pottery, ceramics, fixtures	1,645	35,593	808	13,509	-837	-51	-22,084	-62
327120	Clay building materials	830	36,176	685	21,556	-145	-17	-14,620	-40
327390	Other concrete products	2,647	62,512	2,085	55,829	-562	-21	-6,683	-11
33151	Ferrous, iron, steel foundries	1,124	99,452	731	55,634	-393	-35	-43,818	-44

(continued)

Table 4.2 NAISC Industry data on establishments and employment (continued)

NAISC Code	Industry	2002 Establish	2002 Employ	2023 Establish	2023 Employ	Changes since 2002			
						Establish	%	Employ	%
33152	Nonferrous foundries	1,589	78,936	950	50,309	-639	-40	-28,627	-36
332710	Machine shops	24,773	315,856	19,078	261,340	-5,695	-23	-54,516	-17
33211	Forging and stamping	2,703	119,680	2,258	89,890	-445	-16	-29,790	-25
3322	Cutlery/and hand tools	1,748	54,448	1,424	34,989	-324	-19	-19,459	-36
33261	Hardware—spring and wire	1,861	70,891	1,288	39,776	-573	-31	-31,115	-44
333244	Printing machinery	591	15,890	NA	NA	NA	NA	NA	NA
33331	Commercial service machinery	3,117	128,503	3,155	88,771	38	1	-39,732	-31
3341	Computers/peripherals	2,164	246,993	2,411	159,953	247	11	-87,040	-35
3342	Communications equipment	2,715	183,072	2,876	84,895	161	6	-98,177	-54
3344	Semiconductors	6,670	523,680	7,008	394,014	338	5	-129,666	-25
3346	Magnetic media	1,822	55,707	1,585	10,565	-237	-13	-45,142	-81
333511	Industrial mold manufact	2,935	44,482	1,503	32,324	-1,432	-49	-12,158	-27
333515	Cutting tool accessories	1,448	30,764	1,125	21,021	-323	-22	-9,743	-32
333514	Tool and die and jig fixtures	5,288	83,463	2,646	51,904	-2,642	-50	-31,559	-38
333517	Machine tool manufact	2,171	43,711	2,099	42,744	-72	-3	-967	-2
3353	Electrical equipment	3,112	174,007	3,140	151,951	28	1	-22,056	-13
33522	Major appliance manufacturing	282	72,758	326	51,123	44	16	-21,635	-30
3363	Motor vehicle parts	6,765	728,766	6,424	560,763	-341	-5	-168,003	-23
3371	Household furniture	19,472	398,687	12,768	221,982	-6,704	-34	-176,705	-44

Private Industry by 6-digit NAISC Industry—Annual averages

Source: Bureau of Labor Statistics (DOL).

Note: NAISC INDUSTRY 3344 semiconductors has increased the number of plants due to the Chips Act investment but employemnt has declined from 523.680 in 2002 to 394,014 in 2023 becasue automation has reduced employment needs in the industry.

Why America Must Have a Strong and Growing Manufacturing Sector

Maintain living standards: Cheap imports have not been enough to improve living standards for the majority of the middle class. For all the reasons described in Chapters 2 and 3 too many people are not able to make a wage that covers living costs. Manufacturing is a source of high wage jobs and benefits for workers without college degrees.

Research and development (R&D) and American innovation: President Obama, in a State of the Union speech, summed up our competitive challenge when he said, "The only durable strength we have—the only one that can withstand these gale winds—is innovation." He also said that "maintaining our leadership in research and technology is crucial to America's success."

If innovation is going to be the strategy that keeps America the number one economy, then private research and development is the key—and 68 percent of private R&D comes from manufacturing. The important point is that the majority of innovation and new technologies come from manufacturing—not the service industries. And, when a country loses its capability to manufacture, it loses the ability to innovate. Innovation and manufacturing are inextricably linked.

Exports: In 2024 imports were $4,110.0 billion, and exports were $3,191.6 billion, producing a deficit of $918.4 billion. Sixty-seven percent of our exports are manufactured goods— so if we are going to have any chance of reducing the trade deficit or increasing exports, the only answer is to increase manufacturing and decrease outsourcing. Services are only 27 percent of our exports, so increases of service exports simply won't do it.

Manufacturing is key to our national defense: Ten industries are declining that manufacture products and technologies critical to our defense, such as propellant chemicals, batteries, specialty metals, flat panel displays, semiconductors, printed circuit boards, machine tools and advanced materials. We can't have strong national security if we continue to outsource components and critical materials to low-cost countries. The only way to stop these critical products and technologies from falling into the hands of our competitors is to manufacture them in the United States and for the government to declare some of them critical to national security and off limits to foreign competitors.

Manufacturing is the foundation of global power: From the rise of England in the nineteenth century; to the rise of America, Japan, and Germany in the twentieth century; and the rise of China, Taiwan, and Korea in the twenty-first century: Manufacturing has been the key to the growth and power of each country. The power is not just building factories that manufacture goods; it is making the machinery that makes the goods. The primary point is that to remain a global power, America must have a strong manufacturing base.

No other sector in the economy can achieve these goals. If we want to remain the number one economy in the world, we must do something about the trade deficit and reduce outsourcing. In my opinion, we won't maintain our position as the world's largest economy as a service economy.

Conclusion

According to Jeff Ferry of the CPA,

> The strength of our manufacturing sector from 1870 to 1970, and its tendency to pay high wages to its workers was the single most important factor in national wealth and in our strong middle class. The aim of globalization from 1990 on, was to force US workers to compete with low wage workers around the world.

The resultant deindustrialization has led to the decline of the middle class, and sacrificing jobs, industries, technologies, suppliers and communities. But it is based on hypocrisy. Why should the workers in the lower and middle class be asked to do all of the sacrificing while the multinationals and their shareholders gain all the spoils?

The only answer is to begin protecting our industries and reshoring our products even if consumer prices increase in the short term. Additionally, strategically selected tariffs could help grow the U.S. manufacturing base, protect key industries, reduce dependency on imports, and create good-paying jobs. The new economic policy would improve the middle-class share of income, reduce the rise of populism and frustration, and contribute to the long-term health of the U.S. economy.

The best way to build widespread prosperity and reverse the decline of the middle class is through the growth of domestic manufacturing. Revitalizing U.S. manufacturing is achievable to rebuild the middle class and strengthen the economy. We need a new industrial policy with a goal of achieving manufacturing 15 percent of GDP.

CHAPTER 5

The Disintegration of American Industries

We won't remain the number one economy and a world power if we allow the continued disintegration of American manufacturing industries and transition to the postindustrial service economy.

I have been following manufacturing industries for many years using the Bureau of Labor Statistics database on North American Industry Classification System (NAICS) industries, in terms of the changes in employment and establishments. Those people who think we might be in a manufacturing renaissance because of the digital revolution, need to take another hard look. The data in Table 4.2 show that that 36 out of 38 manufacturing industries have been declining since 2002 in terms of both number of plants and employees. Some of the industries, such as textiles, apparel, and furniture, have lost so many workers, plants, suppliers, and market share, that they are probably beyond recovery.

Most academic economists view the decline of these industries as the natural progression toward a postindustrial economy and are not a cause for alarm. But if we want to someday have a real manufacturing renaissance, we are going to have to address the long-term economic problems causing the decline of our manufacturing industries. The real solution will require reducing the trade deficit, addressing the strong dollar problem, stopping currency manipulation, stopping the mercantilist cheating by China, and developing national program to create a skilled workforce.

President Trump now has the world's attention on these issues with his latest round of tariffs. Perhaps we might build on this momentum and find the political will to protect our industries. Many of these industries also have national security implications and need protection if we are going to maintain a strong defense and our weapons systems.

The Critical Industries That All Manufacturing Industries Depend On

Perhaps the most important skilled workers are the high skill industries, like machine shops, machine tools, mold making, tool and die, cutting tool accessories, semiconductors, forging, stamping, and foundries. These industries are critical to any reshoring initiative or any manufacturing renaissance because they serve all other manufacturing industries. They are critical industries because they are fundamental to the manufacturing process, and are absolutely essential if we are to have a chance at growing domestic manufacturing or making any of President Trump's programs work.

Machine Shops

Machining is a material removal process that is used on metal, plastics, wood, ceramics, and composites. Machining is essential to hundreds of industries and thousands of products as tiny as a machine screw and as large as a turbine bearing for a dam. Machining is absolutely essential for all industrial products but is also used in consumer products to make parts for everything from dishwashers and faucets to cellphones and toys. The machining industry has lost 5,695 shops and 54,516 employees since 2001.

American manufacturers began buying machining services from overseas companies as far back as the 1980s. Many of these companies had moved manufacturing operations overseas, to take advantage of lower prices due to lower labor and operational costs, and then began to use the same overseas machine shops in their domestic operations.

Technological advancements, such as robotics and advanced CNC machines, also led to a decrease in the demand for manual labor. As manufacturing declined, fewer people were entering vocational training programs and apprenticeships. This made it harder for machine shops to find the skilled machinists needed to compete with overseas companies and many shops closed. As sales and profits decreased, smaller shops struggled to invest in advanced technology and equipment upgrades, making it difficult to compete.

Machine Tools

These are the master machines that make other machines and products. Max Holland wrote in his book *When the Machines Stopped*, "Thus at the heart of the industrial health of any nation is its machine tool industry. It is no coincidence that the erosion of the machine tool industry parallels the decline of domestic manufacturing."

In 1965 American machine tool manufacturers had 28% of the world market for machine tools, but today we have 5% of the world market.. The machine tool industry has lost 72 plants (3 percent) and 967 (2 percent) employees since 2001. According to the Modern Machine Shop data, the United States imported $6.2 billion worth of machine tools, and exported $1.5 billion in 2024. This begs an obvious question: Can a manufacturing renaissance occur if most of the machine tools used by industry are imported?

Tool and Die Makers

Tool and die makers are advanced machinists that are critical to manufacturing. They are the highly skilled artisans that make the jigs, fixtures, dies, molds, cutting tools, and gauges used in the manufacturing process. Since globalization began in the 1980s, Asian countries have gone all out to develop more tool and die, mold makers, and advanced machinists. In the United States, however, tool and die makers have lost 2,642 (50 percent) plants and 31,559 (38 percent) employees since 2001. To become a journeyman requires five years 10,000 hours of training.

Industrial Mold Companies

Industrial mold companies lost 1,432 shops (49 percent) and 12,158 workers (27 percent) since 2001. Just as in machining and tool and die, many American manufacturers began buying mold making services and products from Asian countries with lower labor costs. Mold Imports are also coming from Mexico and Canada further decreasing domestic mold production. To become a journeyman in mold making also requires four to five years and 8,000 to 10,000 hours of training, and historically U.S. companies have not invested in training that takes thousands of hours.

Foundries

The process of making parts by pouring metal to make a casting is ubiquitous and is used in the machinery, automotive, pipe, fitting, railroad equipment, valve, and pump industries. Castings are also used in everything from heart valves to aircraft carrier propellers and in every home for bathtubs, sinks, fixtures, and furnaces. The primary driver of this decline is that most American corporations now buy their castings from low-cost countries where there are no environmental regulations and labor is cheap.

Ferrous, Iron, Steel Foundries

The ferrous, iron, steel foundry industry declined by 393 (35 percent) plants and 43,818 (44 percent) employees since 2001? The primary reason is increased competition from Asian countries like China. Domestic manufacturers started buying castings from foreign countries as far back as the 1980s due to lower prices. Some U.S.-based casting producers also invested in foreign operations to supply customers who had moved their manufacturing plants to the foreign country. The industry has also seen a shift to lighter, nonferrous metals such as aluminum, further reducing the demand for traditional iron and steel castings. The industry has also suffered from rising energy costs and fluctuating ferrous scrap prices, along with the problem of finding and keeping skilled workers across various levels.

Nonferrous Foundries

Nonferrous foundries declined by 639 (40) plants and 28,627 (36 percent) employees since 2001? The reasons are the same as the ferrous foundries in that they are faced with increased competition from Asian countries like China. Some U.S.-based casting producers also invested in foreign operations to supply customers who had moved their manufacturing plants to the foreign country. The industry also faced significant competition within the United States, leading to a consolidation of businesses. The industry has also suffered from rising energy costs, the cost of environmental regulations, along with the problem of finding and keeping skilled workers. The foundry industry has also been hit hard by an aging workforce, with many experienced workers retiring, and high turnover rates, which have impacted productivity and knowledge transfer.

Forging and Stamping

Forging and stamping shops declined by 445 (16 percent) plants and 29,790 (25 percent) employees since 2001? The contraction of the forging and stamping industry in the United States began in the 1980s when American companies began buying products and services from foreign countries. From 1979 to 1990, 25 percent of the forging companies in the United States went out of business. The contraction of this industry goes on today Demand for forged and stamped products also declined from major downstream markets like aerospace, agricultural machinery, and oil and gas machinery. The volatile world prices for steel and nonferrous metals have also added to the industry instability, impacting profitability and making them less competitive. As in many other manufacturing industries there has been an ongoing shortage of skilled craftsmen, particularly as older workers retire.

Cutting Tool Accessories

Cutting tool accessories declined by 323 (22 percent) plants and 9,743 (32 percent) employees since 2001 for generally the same reasons that machine shops and machining declined—the rise of international trade and the ability of companies to source cutting tools from countries with lower labor costs, such as China.

These eight industries have lost 10,902 plants and 312,217 highly skilled workers since 2001 (Table 5.1). A big part of these eight critical industries is now offshore, and we have lost the skills, know-how, operational competencies, and many of the highly skilled artisans that make the jigs, fixtures, dies, molds, cutting tools, gauges, castings, forgings,

Table 5.1 *High skill industries that serve other manufacturing industries*

NAISC code	Industry	2023 Establishments	2023 Lost percent	2023 Employment	2023 Lost percent
3344	Semiconductors	+338	+5	–129,666	–25
333511	Industrial mold manufacturing	–1,432	–49	–12,158	–27
333515	Cutting tool accessories	–323	–22	–9,743	–32
333514	Tool and die and jig fixtures	–2,542	–50	–31,559	–38
333517	Machine tool manufacturing	–72	–3	–967	–2
332710	Machine shops	–5,695	–23	–54,516	–17
33211	Forging and stamping	–445	–16	–29,790	–25
33151	Ferrous, iron, steel foundries	–393	–35	–43,818	–44
Total Lost		–10,902		–312,217	

stampings, and the machining used in the manufacturing process of all other manufacturing industries.

The decline of these critical industries begs two questions. First, how can Trump's plan to reshore manufacturing work if these critical support industries continue to decline? Second, where will we find these highly skilled workers? You might be able to steal some skilled workers from competitors, but the pool of workers with these skills no longer exists. Replacing these workers is going to take apprentice-style training, and it takes four years (8,000 hours) to make a journeyman worker from an entry-level applicant. I don't think it can happen unless Congress creates an emergency apprenticeship act with funding.

Paper Industry. The U.S. paper industry has lost 125 establishments (20 percent) and 56,656 (53 percent) employees since 2001. The declining demand for printing and writing paper is primarily due to the shift toward digital communication, online publications, and electronic billing. But the decline is also due to increased competition from Asian producers, high energy costs, and the competition for wood fiber.

The competition from Asian producers, particularly from China, has played a significant role in the decline of the U.S. paper industry. China has become a major global paper exporter, with its share of global paper exports exceeding 15 percent in 2023. Between 1997 and 2007, Asian paper production increased by 76 percent, while North American production declined by 4 percent.

Rubber Industry. The industry has declined by 143 (23 percent) plants and 20,329 (42 percent) workers since 2001. The decline was generally caused by globalization and outsourcing. Specifically, the increased competition from foreign manufacturers has driven down prices and made it difficult for domestic producers to compete. Companies were motivated to shift production overseas due to lower labor costs and less stringent regulations in some regions.

Pottery, ceramics, and tile. The pottery and ceramics industry declined by 837 (51 percent) plants, and 22,084 (62 percent) employees since 2001? The industry makes a wide variety of products from tableware and floor tiles to pipes, bricks, and kiln linings. The primary reason for decline is the inability to compete with lower foreign prices. The U.S. industry has older facilities with obsolete equipment that can't compete with more modern and efficient production methods. These plants have been operated by a majority of unskilled labor and have been vulnerable to strong import competition, especially from countries like China.

Clay and Brick. The clay and brick building materials industry has declined by 145 (17 percent) plants and 14,620 (40 percent) employees since 2001. Foreign Competition and low sea transport costs are the primary reason and imports come from China, Ecuador, Panama as well as Peru, the United Kingdom, and Russia. The United States imports building bricks from several countries including Mexico, Denmark, Italy, Spain, and China. China, has also disrupted the industry with reciprocal tariffs on materials like steel, aluminum, copper, and gypsum, which increased costs for clay brick manufacturing. The industry is also plagued by high energy costs, and environmental regulations: The EPA has implemented regulations to control hazardous air pollutants emitted from kilns and other processes.

Semiconductor Industry

Most U.S. chipmakers made a critical decision years ago: go fabless which means doing the design and marketing in the United States and farming out the production to foreign countries. The United States is the inventor of the semiconductor technology and was once a major chip manufacturing center. But top U.S. chip designers outsourced fabrication to leading-edge processors, mostly to Taiwan, South Korea, and more recently to China. The fabless model slashed operating costs and generated short-term profits. The new business model spurred the rise of fabless chipmakers and chip stocks such as Nvidia (NVDA), Broadcom (AVGO), and Qualcomm (QCOM). But there was a major downside.

Hiring overseas contractors to do their manufacturing had dire long-term consequences for the semiconductor industry. It caused logistics snarls, and critical chip shortages. The Fabless model led to a heavy dependence on the overseas factories of non-U.S. companies for a technology that's critical in many U.S. industries, and for U.S. corporations and their customers, including the U.S. government. Dependence on imported chips has created big national security and technology supply issues.

The required workforce to operate these plants is in short supply and many thousands of new employees must be trained. The CHIPS Act's goal is for the United States to reach 20 percent of global chip manufacturing by 2030, up from 12 percent, but that may prove to be a tough goal to meet.

The important point is that the semiconductor industry got themselves into this problem by outsourcing their production and making themselves and their country dependent on foreign foundries who are also competitors.

The magnetic media industry lost 237 (13 percent) plants and 45,142 (81 percent) employees since 2001. The primary reason was technological change because of the shift from analog to digital recording, particularly in audio and video production, led to a decrease in the demand for magnetic tape. Also, the rise of solid-state drives (SSDs) and cloud storage solutions gradually replaced magnetic storage devices like hard drives and tapes in various applications as their prices dropped significantly. Competition from foreign producers, who have lower production costs also contributed to the overall decline of the industry.

The hardware spring and wire industry lost 573 (31 percent) plants and 31,115 (44 percent) employees since 2001. The primary reason was competition from low-cost imports from Asia. Some countries like China, Japan, India, and South Korea, have both low-price raw material suppliers, and low-price manufacturers. giving them a competitive edge. In the United States, rising prices for raw materials like copper and aluminum, have increased production costs, and in 2023 led to a decline in overall industry sales. It was the first decline since 2008-2009.

The U.S. Communications Equipment Industry (CIC) has been growing because of 5G network expansion, cloud-based communication solutions, increased use of IoT and intelligent devices, and the demand for high-speed Internet and broadband infrastructure. However, the communications industry lost 98,177 employees since 2001 due to the shift toward wireless communication, automation, software, cloud-based solutions and outsourcing.

The Telecom industry imports many communication products and in 2020 the communications and information industry had a $247 billion deficit. China is the largest foreign supplier of the Internet of Things (IOT) equipment to the United States. In 2018, IOT imports from China totaled $157 billion or 60 percent of the total IOT imports.

In 2019, President Trump issued an executive order to secure the IOT supply chain because purchasing these products from foreign countries was considered a national security risk. The executive order said that "foreign adversaries are increasingly creating and exploiting vulnerabilities in information and communications technology and services, in order to commit malicious cyber-enabled actions, including economic and industrial espionage against the United States and its people."

Autos—Since 1980, the American auto manufacturers' share of their own market has declined significantly. In 1980, they held about 84 percent of the market, but by 2025 that share had fallen to around 40 percent of the U.S. new vehicle market. This decline is attributed to the rise foreign automakers like Honda, Toyota, and others, who offered fuel-efficient and reliable cars, and challenged the dominance of the Big Three (GM, Ford, Chrysler). While foreign automakers were embracing new technologies and systems like lean production and quality control systems, the Big Three struggled to adopt them, leading to higher production costs and less competitive vehicles. In addition, consumers started shifting toward smaller, more fuel-efficient vehicles, which was not a strong suit for the American Big Three at the time. The "Big Three" automakers (General Motors, Ford, and Chrysler) have shed approximately 600,000 U.S. jobs since 1980.

Class 8 trucks—Class 8 trucks are defined as those that haul between 33,001 and 80,000 pounds. In 2022, U.S. Class 8 truck production totaled over 320,000 units. It is a large industry and supports hundreds of thousands of jobs.

Three of the four major Class 8 truck manufacturers in the United States are owned by foreign companies. They are Daimler Trucks North America (owned by the German company Daimler); Mack Trucks (owned by The Volvo Group, a Swedish company), and PACCAR (owned by DAF Trucks, a Dutch company). The fourth major manufacturer, Navistar International Corporation, is owned by a U.S.-based company, but it is a subsidiary of the (Volkswagen Group a German company).

According to S&P Global Mobility, a division of S&P Global, which provides data, forecasts, and analyses for the commercial vehicle industries, more than 40 percent of Class 8 trucks in the United States are imported from Canada and Mexico. The United States–Mexico–Canada Agreement (USMCA), which replaced NAFTA, provides for duty-free trade of most goods between the three countries, including Class 8 trucks. This could change if the United States decides they don't meet the USMCA origin requirements, or if Trump decides that the United States needs to reduce import dependency because it jeopardizes transport and infrastructure safety. According to the CPA, "China linked parts and components are re-entering the United States in trucks built in Mexico." This has national security implications along with the fact that 70 percent of Class 8 truck sales in the United States are controlled by foreign OEMs.

The Trump Tariff program is constantly changing and on October 17, 2025, Trump formalized a new 25 percent tariff on imported medium- and heavy-duty trucks and parts as a result of the Section 232 probe into imported trucks. The 25 percent tariff would only apply to the non-U.S. content of vehicles and parts imported under the USMCA, after a process is established to determine and apply tariffs to their non-U.S. components.

Millwork and wood floors—This industry lost 884 (34 percent) plants and 26,739 (45 percent) employees since 2001. The primary reason is importing competition and the increased importation of wood products, particularly from countries like China. The United States has become a leading importer of softwood lumber, partly due to mill closures. Environmental concerns in the early 1990s led to a drop in timber harvests from federal lands, reducing raw material for mills and impacting employment.

Automation and new technologies have made lumber mills less labor-intensive, leading to job losses even when harvest levels stabilized. Larger companies benefit more from advanced automation due to economies of scale, while smaller firms may struggle to justify such investments. When sales and profits are declining manufacturers can't afford investments in new technology.

Cutlery and hand tools—This industry has lost 324 plants (19 percent) and 19,459 (36 percent) employees since 2001. Intense competition, leading to price wars and margin pressures. The primary cause is Globalization and companies moving production offshore to countries with lower labor costs. Automation and robotics, has also reduced the number of workers. Fluctuations in the prices of raw materials, such as steel and alloys, have impacted production costs and lightweight, durable materials like aluminum and titanium, required new investment which is difficult when sales and profits are down. Also, the pressures on sustainability and to adopt eco-friendly technologies has impacted costs.

Commercial and Service Industry Machinery—This industry includes a wide range of equipment such as automatic vending machines, commercial laundry and dry-cleaning equipment, office machinery, photographic and photocopying equipment, and commercial-type cooking equipment. The industry has lost 38 plants (1 percent) and 39,732 (31 percent) employees since 2001. Competition from countries like China and India has contributed to the closure of manufacturing facilities in the United States and the shift in production to new manufacturing plants in other countries. There has also been a decline in demand and deteriorating market conditions caused by economic uncertainty, global disruptions caused by events like the COVID-19 pandemic and international conflicts, coupled with factors like rising interest rates and inflation.

Shipbuilding—During World War II, the U.S. shipyard labor force of 750,000 people was employed in an industry that built 9,000 ships in six years. According to the MaRad Bureau of labor Statistics the U.S. ship building and repairing industry had 178,000 workers in 1980. Employment declined to 105,517 in 2023.

Today the industry builds less than 10 vessels for oceangoing commerce in a typical year. In comparison, China builds over a thousand such ships each year. In the 1950s, U.S. merchant marine transported a third of all global trade. Today the entire U.S.-registered fleet of oceangoing commercial ships numbers fewer than 200 vessels, out of a global total of 44,000 or 0.004 percent. From a national security perspective the U.S. merchant marine today, may not be able to support military sealift requirements in a war.

The U.S. Navy is not keeping up with China in military shipbuilding. After 2001, the U.S. Navy fleet size decreased from 316 to 278 ships. The Navy's fleet size was 296 ships as of January 2025. China now has the largest fleet of warships in the world—approximately 350 ships. In 2026 the Navy expects to build only four combat vessels, a level of effort that if sustained would guarantee Chinese maritime dominance by 2030.

Shipbuilding is a classic example of how offshoring industries can lead to national security issues and then force Congress to have to legislate emergency federal programs to counter the threat. The same thing happened with semiconductors and we didn't react until the shortages began closing auto production lines.

Bipartisan leaders in the House and Senate have introduced the Ships for America Act. This act would establish a 25 percent investment tax credit for shipyard investments as well as an investment in maritime workforce development, with the goal of expanding the U.S. flag international fleet of 250 ships in 10 years and growing local economies.

Congress's polarized political system under Donald Trump doesn't seem to know whether they should cut federal programs or tariff foreign countries. If the Trump administration doesn't support shipbuilding it could result in closer of more U.S. shipyards.

Spectacular Industry Losses—Textile and Apparel Industries

Between 1979 and 2019, these industries lost over 1.8 million jobs, going from 2.2 million to 334,000 employees, according to the Bureau of Labor Statistics. This represents a job loss of 81 percent. Since the late 1990s, more than 200,000 textile manufacturing jobs in the United States have been lost, and 650 textile plants in the United States were closed.

The textile and apparel industries are probably too far gone to be saved and are examples of what will happen to the other industries described in this chapter unless they get some form of protection.

Conclusion

The decline of U.S. shipbuilding is just one facet of America's ongoing deindustrialization. We have gradually watched over the disintegration of industries from computers and smartphones to aluminum and copy paper. The disintegration of our industries has been the result of

America's free trade policy while our competitors used tariffs and trade barriers. We opened the flood gates to our foreign competitors and the result was a huge increase in imports and trade deficits. The declining industry problem has been exacerbated by rising energy costs, environmental regulations, lack of skilled labor and training, and lack of investment.

So, the big question is, can the United States afford to allow our industries to continue to deteriorate until we are totally dependent on imports, or is it in our best long-term interests to protect selected industries? If the answer is protection, then how will we do it?

My argument is that we must protect specific industries because:

1. We won't remain the number one economy and a world power if we allow the continued disintegration of American manufacturing industries and transition to the postindustrial service economy.
2. We can't maintain national security and weapon systems if materials like aluminum, steel, and rare earth have shortages and cannot be controlled by the United States?
3. We can't do anything about shortages as long as outsourcing continues and critical products and materials are imported from foreign countries.
4. Similarly, we are subject to rogue countries like China using shortages as leverage for price manipulation, political negotiation, and extortion as long as critical products and materials are imported.
5. If industries continue to decline then American workers will always be compared to foreign wages and wages will continue to decline. Unless we can find a way to protect and grow wages, the middle class will continue to decline.
6. If the answer is protection, the government should make a priority list of critical products and key manufacturing industries that need to be protected.
7. If not tariffs then what is the answer? Without tariffs, how can we stop the erosion of our industries and the loss of technologies?

CHAPTER 6

The Backlash and Election of Donald Trump

The backlash was very evident in the 2024 presidential election, when the middle class voted for their pocketbook.

The American middle class has been on the decline since 1980, and the prosperity they once enjoyed is also declining because of rising consumer prices and stagnant wages. Coincident with the decline of the middle class was the rise of globalism—the global flow of goods, services, and capital. For decades globalism and free trade have been the foundational strategy of governments and multinational corporations (MNCs). Unfortunately, Globalization led to deindustrialization, redistribution of wealth, stagnant wages, the decline of living standards, insecurity not experienced for generations, and left many of the losers behind.

Supporters of globalization and free trade argued it would eventually raise living standards, but after four decades, middle-class citizens in most Western societies have awakened to the fact that it isn't happening, and they view globalization as a threat and a trap. Globalism's success has led to a crisis of governability and political breakdown between electorates in the United States and Europe who want change on economic, political, and cultural issues. Voters in industrialized democracies are particularly interested in their governments dealing with the decline of living standards, growing inequality, immigration, climate change, and a variety of cultural issues.

There has been a titanic shift against globalization illustrated by the election of Donald Trump, Brexit in the UK, the rise of right-wing parties in Europe, and the Trump administration's new tariff program. The latter is viewed as a hostile act against the globalized order, and an attempt by the United States to remake global order.

Election of Trump

In the 2024 presidential election, 56 percent of voters without college degrees supported Trump, including union and blue-collar workers in Michigan, Pennsylvania, and Wisconsin. Harris beat Trump among college-educated White voters by 67 percent to 32 percent but there were many more voters without a college degree. Trump's populist approach to trade, **manufacturing, and job protection, resonated strongly with working-class voters.** Trump courted working class whites by promising the restoration of the old industrial economy–through negotiated trade deals and tariffs on imports,. by pledging to deport immigrants, which he said would reduce competition for native born workers, and by promising rapid economic growth from tax cuts, deregulation and more drilling.[1]

During the election, Kamala Harris tried to tell working-class people that the economy during the Biden administration had been strong, but it didn't work. Harris's speeches seldom mentioned both the middle-class wage problems and the decline of manufacturing. However, inflation, rising costs, and stagnant wages were the biggest problem faced by the middle class, and blue-collar workers had reservations about Kamala Harris's ability to understand their problems or change the economy.

On the other hand, Donald Trump was boisterous, belligerent, and bombastic, and made promises and guarantees to working-class people with his Make America Great Again message. In the eyes of working-class voters, he was a man of action who would implement change.

The Democratic Party problem goes back to Clinton's 1993 election campaign when he convinced the party to favor college-educated workers. But the last election proved that depending on the college educated who endorse culturally progressive values and prioritized social causes over economic interests was a mistake.

A Penn State labor and employment relations professor, Paul Clark said, "You can look at the data in terms of income that defines working-class voters. In the 2008 election, Obama got 63 percent of voters making less than $50,000, and McCain got 35 percent. That's a 28 percent margin. In 2012, Obama got 60 percent but the margin fell to 22 percent. In 2024, Harris

---

[1] Jim Tankersley, How Trump won: The revenge of working-class whites, Nov.9,2017, The Washington Post.

got 48.5 percent and Trump 49 percent, meaning that between 2008 and 2024, the Democrats lost almost 30 percent of working-class voters. And that's enough to explain the voters making less than $50,000 a year."

Senator Bernie Sanders of Vermont said, "it should come as no great surprise that a Democratic Party which has abandoned working-class people find that the working class has abandoned them."

President Trumps victory over Kamala Harris in 2024 reflects a society in transition with key cultural, political, demographic shifts that led to a voter backlash. The backlash was very evident in the 2024 presidential election, when the middle class voted their pocketbook.

The Growth of Inequality

Figure 6.1 shows that since 1980 the 1 percent have had an incredible increase in their percentage of national income. This is a growth of 162 percent since 1980. At the same time the bottom 50 percent declined from 21 to 13 percent, creating a big rise in inequality.

The bottom 50 percent have been suffering the most from rising costs and stagnant wages. They see the obvious inequality, where they are struggling and everybody else above them on the chart is doing well to

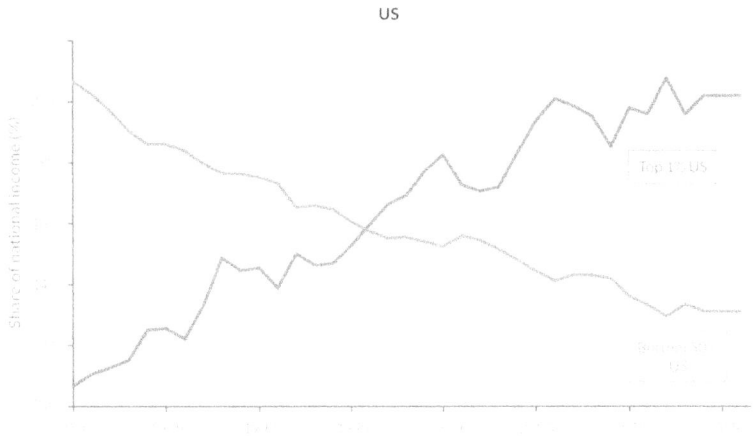

Figure 6.1 The growth of inequality since 1980

Source: Global Inequality Dynamics: New Findings from WID.world" Authors: Facundo Alvaredo, Lucas Chancel, Thomas Piketty, Emmanuel Saez, Gabriel Zucman Publication: American Economic Review: Papers and Proceedings, May 2017

exceedingly well, while they suffer. Many Americans connect globalization with inequality, particularly the growth of income for the top 10 percent of society who have benefited enormously from globalization while leaving most of the middle class behind.

The Rise of Populism

Globalization, inequality, deindustrialization, and the decline of the middle class has led to waves of populism across the United States and many countries in Europe. Right-wing political parties have used the economic problems caused by deindustrialization and Globalization to increase their vote shares in Italy, Hungary, France, Poland, Greece, Germany, and Sweden led by new populist leaders like Viktor Orbán, Marine Le Pen, Norbert Hofer, Nigel Farage, and Geert Wilders. Their rise in popularity is generally a reaction to globalization, free trade, immigration, wage stagnation, and multiculturalism. There is also a rise in religious fundamentalism in Buddhism, Christianity, Islam, and Hinduism—which parallels political nationalism. Populism is most simply defined as a support of the concerns of ordinary people on the right and left of the political spectrum. Both groups claim they represent the majority's interests, and most often are against a privileged elite.

Populism has become a class struggle where the unrest has often led to an attraction to authoritarian figures, who offer simplistic solutions. Populists and extremists rely on strategies to nurture fear, alienation, and discontent, attracting attention with promises to restore the nation to some former glory or to the values of the past. The American Dream seems frozen in time, and a relic of the belief that every generation would exceed the gains of the previous generation.

Economic Factors

Many postelection surveys in 2025 indicate that the number one problem for working-class and union workers is inflation and the cost of living. Both political parties brag about how the economy is strong. They cite the low unemployment rate of 4 percent, booming stock market, quantity of new jobs created. But the strong economy masks the fact that many citizens are not sharing in the benefits of the strong economy, and the fact that millions of workers are not making enough income to cover living expenses.

A survey by the National True Cost of Living Coalition found that "two thirds, 65 percent, of middle-class Americans said they were struggling financially and didn't expect their situation to improve for the rest of their lives."

Anti-globalism sentiment is most obvious in regions hit hardest like the Midwest (heartland) and parts of the South. As globalization and outsourcing closed plants in these regions, many towns and cities entered a downward spiral of unemployment, under employment, and the erosion of the local economic base which affects all citizens, businesses, and merchants in the local area. The effects on these communities are still apparent today, and many of these people feel powerless, angry, and worried about their future, which has led to a rise in populism and a polarized society. The voters in these regions were more likely to vote for Trump in the 2024 election.

Employment and wages—The plight of working people and the middle class in America is revealed when you examine the BLS statistics of hourly wages and annual incomes. The following chart (Table 6.1) from the Bureau of Labor Statistics—occupational employment and wage statistics—validates the claim of wages not keeping up with inflation.

Table 6.1 shows that 50 percent of the workforce (82 million workers) make less than $20 per hour or $41,600 per year. If you examine the cost of the three H's (health care, home, and higher education) it is obvious that a family earning $41,600 per year will be struggling financially. The BLS table also shows that 25 percent (41 million people) are living on wages of $15 per hour. This group is considered poor or low wage.

Table 6.1 Occupational Employment and Wages

Percentile	10%	25%	50%	75%	90%
Hourly Wage	$11.00	$15.00	$20.00	$24.00	$29.00
Annual Wage	$22,899	$31,200	$41,600	$49,920	$60,320

Source: Bureau of Labor Statistics, Occupational Employment and wage statistics

Table 6.2 Real wage trends from 1979 to 2018

Education Group	10th percentile	50th percentile	90th percentile
College Degree	4%	14.40%	34.30%
High school or less	−3.70%	−12.70%	−9.70%

Source: Bureau of Labor Statistics, Occupational Employment and wage statistics

The inflation-adjusted wage trends in Table 6.2 for the work force as a whole show that college-educated workers have held their own since 1979, but workers with a high school education or less have declined in real terms in the top, middle, and bottom of the wage distribution. Wage trends from 1979 to 2018 show which people are making it financially and which are not. Wage gains are the primary lever for raising living standards. The data comes from the Current Population Survey and does not include nonwage compensation such as employer-provided health insurance, paid leave, or retirement contribution.

Economic inequality has led to social, political, and economic divisions making it harder for society to function and poses a threat of future instability. A shrinking middle-class has also led to widespread economic hardship which has led to anger, resentment, frustration, and a sense of no future. Unless the country can provide better jobs, higher wages, and reduced inequality there is a risk of political extremism and nondemocratic radical solutions.

Cultural Factors

Deindustrialization leads to economic problems, which leads to wage stagnation, fear and general unrest. The economic problems caused by deindustrialization also lead to cultural changes such as the fear of immigration. It has aroused in many white voters (particularly citizens from the political right) a broad backlash that demands a more restrictive immigration policy, more punitive criminal justice policies, and less generous public spending on immigrants and the poor.

Many conservative voters are reacting against progressive cultural changes in lifestyle like transgender equality, same-sex marriage, racial issues, abortion, and multiculturalism (which is the view that cultures, and ethnicities, particularly those of minority groups, deserve special acknowledgment of their differences within a dominant political culture). The conservative backlash is about eliminating everything from critical race theory and DEI (which stands for diversity, equity, and inclusion) to canceling public broadcasting and Dr. Seuss. It is a realignment of American politics along cultural and educational lines and away from class and income divisions that defined the two parties for much of the twentieth century.

A 2021 report on deindustrialization and white voter backlash by Leonardo Baccini and Stephen Weymouth[2] argues that deindustrialization threatens dominant group status, leading some white voters in affected localities to favor candidates they believe will address economic distress and defend racial hierarchy. The report shows that "whites associated manufacturing job losses with the loss of upward mobility and with a broader American Decline." I think that this problem is predominantly an economic problem facing white high school-educated Americans who have been left behind in the new service economy. Many working Americans believe that upward mobility is no longer valid and the deck is stacked against the average citizen. The people who have been abandoned by America and were the victims of globalization have reason to be resentful and angry.

Polarization

The divide in cultural, political, and economic issues has polarized the country. We seem to have lost the American ability to listen to one another and to compromise. People view themselves as part of the red team or the blue team and act accordingly. Social media accentuates the red team/blue team phenomena by helping people to communicate with other people like themselves, instead of listening and understanding an opposing view.

Populism and polarization can also be described as the posttruth period where objective facts are less important than emotion and personal beliefs. This is most obvious in the public's reaction to science over the last two decades, when many middle-class citizens no longer believe in the science behind evolution, climate change, and vaccination. In health care, this post truth period has led to strong belief in homeopathy, magnetic healing, detoxification, therapeutic touch, and a host of therapies not based on scientific proof.

My favorite female writer, Wendy Kaminer says, "Rationalism is founded on skepticism—a commitment to testing all beliefs, including your own—and the capacity to tolerate doubt. People hungry for absolutes are more likely to choose supernaturalism or unadulterated emotionalism over any system of free inquiry."

---

[2]Leonard Baccini, McGill University, Stephen Weymouth, Georgetown University, 2021, Gone for Good: Deindustrialization, White Voter Backlash, and US Presidential Voting, American Political Science Review.

The issues caused by the transition to a postindustrial service economy, the decline of manufacturing, postmodernism, the information explosion, the introduction of the Internet, new technologies, skepticism of science, and the election of Donald Trump, converged into a distorted reality. The confluence of all of these factors has led to populism and a polarized society. Some writers refer to the development of these trends in the last 30 years as the age of endarkenment where truth weakened and dogma and irrationality became more respectable.

Conclusion

The Trump tariff program shows that the United States is moving away from the post-WWII policies of free trade and low tariffs. In many ways, we are also moving away from our commitment to international cooperation. We are forcing other countries and regions to adjust to a new global reality. Who knows where it will lead?

Many European countries have been more successful than the United States in addressing the problems caused by globalization because they offer strong safety nets for their citizens. They offer a better distribution of income, unemployment insurance, universal health care, and guaranteed pension.

The policies needed to provide a compelling alternative to populism and polarization are difficult to define much less politically implement. If we can't find a way to minimize polarization, there are signs that social discord might accelerate and get out of hand. I believe that the number one threat to constitutional government is the continued decline of the middle class.

We are currently a polarized country where negotiation and compromise seem to be a low priority. The anger and frustration by much of the middle class has led to a backlash. There are many reasons, but I think that inequality, rising prices and stagnant wages are the primary forces.

Few working people, however, understand that the driving force behind all of these economic and political changes are the inequities caused by globalism and free trade. Some economists believe that the answer is to increase the minimum wage and increase the government safety net. But, in my opinion, the long-term answer for many people in the middle class is to stop the deindustrialization of America and rebuild American Manufacturing. To shift the economy to production rather than consumption. If we are to have a chance of reducing inequality and reindustrializing the country, the United States needs a more robust industrial policy that protects key industries, manufacturing jobs, based on selective use of tariffs and an industrial policy with a general goal of increasing manufacturing's share of GDP to at least 15 percent.

Perhaps the best solution is for millions of workers who are struggling financially to vote out their congressional representatives and elect politicians that are more sympathetic to the middle-class problems.

CHAPTER 7

Protecting Our Technologies

How many technologies and industries are we willing to lose, before we lose our ability to compete using innovation as our primary strategy?

Economists and politicians continue to believe innovation is crucial for future American growth and competitiveness. Innovation is a vital strategy because it drives productivity gains, creates new industries, and boosts the overall economy. They also make the case that by investing in research, development, and education, the United States can build a stronger foundation for future innovation, leading to sustained economic growth and improved living standards.

I think everyone believes in an innovation strategy because the United States was the preeminent leader in technologies and inventions for much of the twentieth century. It was Vannevar Bush, who was the Dean of Engineering at MIT and a top military science administrator during World War II, who came up with the idea of using an assemblage of government, private corporations, and research universities as an innovation development triangle to drive innovation. The tripartite idea produced the first computer in 1945, the transistor in 1947, and the Internet in 1983, which became the basis for our modern economy.

The United States went on to develop and patent the microwave oven, defibrillator, compiler, bar code, hard disk drive, industrial robot, video tape, integrated circuit, electronic spreadsheet, light-emitting diodes, plasma display, compact disc, hand calculator, laser printer, microprocessor, magnetic resonance imaging (MRI), global positioning system, mobile phone, digital camera, Gore-Tex, and personal computers. America was really on an innovation roll and thought itself invincible.

The Problem

A strategy of Innovation is a noble idea, but the supporters of an innovation strategy ignore the fact that most of the technologies invented in the United States since World War II are no longer manufactured in America. So, American companies did the research and development of the original products, but then allowed them to be manufactured in foreign countries. The accepted premise can be described as "innovate here–manufacture there." We are slowly losing our technologies to our foreign competitors through technology transfer agreements and outsourcing We have gambled that we can manufacture the technologies in foreign countries and maintain control of the technology and markets over the long term, but the gamble is not working out.

Economists and other supporters of outsourcing didn't realize, or didn't accept, that when manufacturing is outsourced the R&D goes with it. Another way of saying it, is when manufacturing declines innovation also declines or "manufacture there means innovate there" The two are inextricably linked. From a competitive standpoint the decline of American manufacturing has led to a slow decline of innovation.

The same process goes on today, but we are now not only losing the technologies but losing whole industries. Outsourcing by American companies has destroyed our manufacturing base and our capacity to develop new products and technologies.

This scenario begs the obvious question. *How many technologies and industries are we willing to lose, before we lose our ability to compete using innovation as our primary strategy?* There is now considerable evidence that new technologies which were invented in the United States and then manufactured in a foreign country, will lead to losing control of the technology and the market. If we can't reverse this trend then, the strategy of innovation everyone is counting on for the future, is not going to happen.

There is also financial pressure on corporate boards by activist shareholders to reduce domestic R&D costs at multinational corporations (MNCs) like Boeing, Timken, Dupont, Sara Lee, and United Technologies to increase short term profits, and stock prices. A good example is Dupont Chemical. A hedge fund called Trian Fund Management purchased enough Dupont stock to become its fifth-largest share-holder. Trian said publicly it wanted Dupont to double its share price and cut $4 billion from its business. Dupont submitted, cutting 5,000 people from their workforce, including 1,700 from their R&D lab. Dupont's share price climbed 210 percent between 2009 and 2015. We are outsourcing much of our R&D and are reducing domestic R&D through cost reduction and short-term profit goals.

Before drawing any conclusions about innovation, perhaps it is appropriate to first examine the pros and cons of outsourcing.

Pros:
- **Cost Reduction:** The most significant driver for outsourcing was the potential to lower production costs, particularly labor expense, by leveraging cheaper labor in other countries.
- **Access to Global Talent:** Outsourcing allowed companies to tap into a wider pool of skilled workers and expertise,
- **Increased Flexibility:** Outsourcing provided companies with greater flexibility in adjusting production capacity and responding to changes in demand, allowing them to scale up or down quickly as needed.
- **Resource Optimization:** Outsourcing helped companies optimize their resources by freeing up internal staff to focus on core activities and reducing the need for capital investments in equipment and infrastructure.

Cons:
- **Loss of Intellectual Property (IP)**—Outsourcing to a foreign contractor means giving them your technology secrets in order for them to manufacture the product and there is no guarantee that your IP will be protected.
- **Loss of Control**—Outsourcing can lead to loss of control over the engineering, design, developmental process, IP, and eventually allow the contractor to develop their own competitive product and loss of the market and customers.
- **Cost Reduction**—Accessing low-cost foreign labor is now in question since Trump is assessing tariffs on almost all foreign

countries, forcing many manufacturers to either reshore production or find a different low-cost country. U.S. companies could become gypsies moving from one low wage country to another.

- **Global Talent**—Depending on global talent paradoxically meant U.S. corporations could reduce the cost of recruiting and training workers domestically. This has led to an ongoing shortage of skilled workers going back to 1990.
- **Resource Optimization**—The claim that outsourcing has freed internal staff is simply not true if the company closes the U.S. plant and lays everybody off.
- **Time to Market**—It takes longer to make changes to products that are manufactured abroad, so companies are slower to respond to changing market demands—assuming the market is the United States, not the foreign country.
- **Losing Customers**—Some customers prefer products and services manufactured in the United States with local service.
- **Dependency**—As the foreign plant gains more and more production, it will create a dependency and the foreign contractor will gain leverage over the product.
- **Loss of Control**—The biggest long-term threat to the American company is loss of control of both the technology and the market. So, the gamble is to satisfy shareholders with immediate cost reduction and increased profits, but with chance of losing the product and the market in the long term. Outsourcing technologies can create a foreign competitor who knows all of your product secrets, and the probability of creating their own competitive product line after several years.

Most economists have been supportive of outsourcing from the beginning. They consider the migration to low wage countries as a natural outcome of the theory of comparative advantage which says a country should specialize in the things they can produce more efficiently and import the products they cannot produce efficiently. This is a naïve economic notion which ignores the problem of a low wage foreign competitor who will always have an advantage over a high wage country. In addition, the foreign competitor can use currency manipulation to keep the U.S. dollar overvalued so that their imports will always be low priced and our exports priced too high. This academic theory of comparative advantage has not worked for America and we have lost industries, jobs, and technologies as a result.

Outsourcing Patterns

I have been watching outsourcing since the 1980s, and there seems to be a pattern in what happens to the industries and companies:

1. It begins with a U.S. corporation seeking a cost advantage and better short-term profits by outsourcing a product (or parts of a product) to a foreign country.
2. Once the corporation realizes the cost advantage, its competitors follow suit to try and stay competitive in the market.
3. The foreign manufacturer is free to find their own suppliers and sources of materials, eliminating U.S. suppliers from the supply chain.
4. Most people don't realize that along with the product, research and development, the critical knowledge, skills, tools, and process engineering also leave with the product.
5. After a time, foreign manufacturers (or the foreign country) are not satisfied with just making the parts and begin to seek higher value-added work or a greater share of the total product and move toward complete product assembly and management of the whole supply chain.
6. Once the foreign manufacturer has enough experience, they can do the design engineering and design a competitive product that is superior to the original product. Once they have the manufacturing expertise, design capability, and perhaps a competitive product line they no longer need the U.S. OEM and take over the market.

A good example is the electronics industry particularly industries like color televisions, VCRs, and cordless telephones. These products were some of the first to be outsourced to Asian countries, beginning in the 1960s, Today, if you want to buy a television all of the name brands are foreign companies, and come from Japan, Korea, China, and other Asian countries. These countries not only manufacture the complete product but control the technology and market.

Another example was IBM and the first personal computers. Several years after the introduction of its personal computer in 1981, IBM had serious competition from smaller PC makers like Apple, Tandy, Compaq, and Dell and there was growing pressure on its margins. It made a deal with its Chinese distributor Lenovo to make its PCs in China. In a short period of time Lenovo's name was on the nameplate and IBM lost the market, and was out of the personal computer business.

Another example is the semiconductor. The first monolithic IC chip was invented by Robert Noyce of Fairchild Semiconductor in 1958. Robert Noyce and Gordon Moore, left Fairchild Semiconductor to form a new company focused on semiconductor memory and innovation. That company was, Intel, founded on July 18, 1968. In 1971, Intel developed the 4004 electronically programmable microprocessor, which was a major breakthrough that contributed to the rise of the modern digital age.

But as the semiconductor industry grew, many of the companies adopted the fabless model. The fabless model in semiconductor chip manufacturing refers to companies that design and market chips but outsource their production to foreign foundries. Companies, like Qualcomm and Nvidia, focus on design, development, and marketing, while foundries like TSMC and Global Foundries handle the actual chip fabrication. This model allows companies to avoid the high capital costs and complexities of building and operating their own chip fabrication facilities. Outsourcing than saw the U.S. semiconductor manufacturing capacity drop significantly from 37 percent in 1990 to 12 percent today, while China is actively increasing its domestic semiconductor production.

The U.S. reliance on foreign suppliers, particularly in East Asia, introduces risks to national security and supply chain stability. During the COVID-19 pandemic, the U.S. auto industry faced a microchip shortage primarily due to a surge in demand for electronics, coupled with a sharp initial decrease in auto production. When auto production resumed, the auto industry found it was competing with other industries, like consumer electronics, for limited chip supplies, causing delays and production disruptions.

From a short-term profit point of view, it seems perfectly reasonable that most semiconductor manufacturing, which began in the United States, is now done elsewhere. But since 88 percent of microprocessor production is now overseas, the United States lost control of the supply chain, the technology, and deliveries.

Intel, who had been the leader in America's semiconductor industry began having problems and delays in its 10 nm product, a delay that cost the company the substantial technological lead in semiconductor manufacturing it had enjoyed for decades. The company has also been having trouble at the subsequent 7 nm node as well. Intel began talking about giving up on process technology and outsourcing some of its products to its arch rival Taiwan Semiconductor. The big question is, what will happen if a big player in the industry like Intel gives up its engineering expertise? The probable answer is that the industry will pay a horrible price for it down the road.

Foreign semiconductor manufacturers have a big advantage over American manufacturers, because their countries offer substantial subsidies, which have placed the United States at a competitive disadvantage in attracting new fab construction. In addition, federal investment in semiconductor research has been flat, while other governments have invested substantially in research initiatives to strengthen their own semiconductor capabilities.

In 2020, Bob Swan, the CEO of Intel, wrote a letter to President Biden urging a national strategy to support the semiconductor industry. The letter emphasized domestic manufacturing, the need to counter China, and said:

> By investing boldly in domestic semiconductor manufacturing incentives and research initiatives, President Biden and Congress can reinvigorate the U.S. economy and job creation, strengthen national security and semiconductor supply chains, and ensure the U.S. remains the leader in the game-changing technologies of today and tomorrow.

President Biden signed the CHIPS and Science Act in August 2022 in an attempt to revitalize U.S. semiconductor manufacturing. The $52 billion

CHIPS and Science Act is supposed to correct those problems, and has resulted in investment in new semiconductor fabs. These programs are slowly moving ahead. Intel is building two new fabs near Columbus, Ohio, while TSMC is expanding its operations in Arizona with multiple new facilities. Micron is also building a new campus in Clay, New York, and a new fab in Boise, Idaho. Texas Instruments announced plans to invest more than $60 billion in seven semiconductor fabs in Utah and Texas.

It is ironic that the industry who had favored the fabless model and outsourcing, was now petitioning the government for a bailout based on the need for domestic manufacturing. The industry got itself into trouble by outsourcing and reduced investment in R&D and capital investment, gave me pause, and made me rethink the whole idea of an innovation strategy which outsourced our technologies. I concluded that America's multinational corporation's pursuit of short-term profits and outsourcing was a short-term answer that led to devastating long-term results where they would lose the technology and the market.

The Advanced Technology Industries

The Advanced Technology Industries (ATIs), are industries that are at the forefront of economic growth. The sector includes 50 industries: 35 manufacturing, three energy, and 12 service industries. They range from oil and gas to aerospace, biotechnology, life sciences, opto-electronics, communication, weapons, computer systems, nanotechnology, and software. They also include the disruptive technologies, which are innovations that significantly change how consumers, industries, or businesses operate, such as additive manufacturing, advanced materials, advanced robotics, big data analytics, cloud computing, and the Internet of Things.

Why Are They Important? ATIs are very important to the American economy because they are our best shot at maintaining competitive advantage against foreign competitors and succeeding with an innovation strategy. You would think that the contribution of the Advanced Industries is so vital that the government would go all out to protect them. But it didn't and there are big problems emerging.

According to the Brookings Institute,

These industries employ more than 9.5 million workers. U.S. advanced industries produce $2.7 trillion in value added annually—17 percent of all U.S. gross domestic product (GDP). That is more than any other sector, including healthcare, finance, or real estate. At the same time, the sector employs 80 percent of the nation's engineers; performs 90 percent of private-sector R&D; generates approximately 85 percent of all U.S. patents; and accounts for 60 percent of U.S. exports.[1]

We are running deficits—A study by the Information and Technology Foundation (ITF) finds that since 1995 the U.S. global market share in the advanced industries has fallen 6 percent. The ITF also found that that the 36 sectors of the ATI shed 734,000 jobs from 2001 to 2019.[2]

As the following chart shows, America has been running deficits in the ATIs since 2000, and the 2024 deficit was $298 billion. There are many reasons we are running trade deficits in advanced technology products but chief among them are currency manipulation. competitor tariffs, trade barriers, and outsourcing the products by America's MNCs (Figure 7.1).

Currency manipulation—A leading cause of U.S. trade deficits is currency manipulation and dollar misalignment by China and 15 other trading countries.

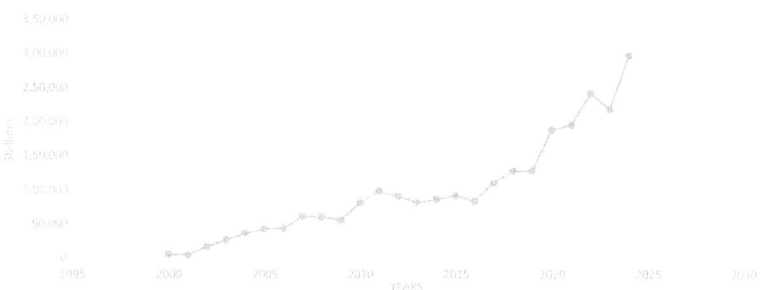

Figure 7.1 The Advanced Technology Industries Trade Deficit

---

[1]Muro, Rothwell, Andes, Fikri, and Kulkarni, February 2015, America's Advanced Industries, The Brookings Institution.
[2]Mark Muro and Yang You. September 7,2023, The nation's advanced industries are falling behind, Brookings Institute, Washington D.C.

Trade deficits—The primary reason for the increase in ATI trade deficits is the outsourcing of technology production. American manufacturers do the R&D to invent these new technologies but then move the production to foreign countries to lower their production costs. According to Alliance for American Manufacturing, American High-Tech companies that supply computers, software, routers, and printers like Microsoft, Intel, Hewlett Packard, IBM, Dell, and Cisco "rely on Chinese factories for an average of 51 percent of the components used to make their products" This is a problem for two reasons. First, their imports increase the deficit in Advanced Technology products. Second, it gives foreign countries our technologies, and means our competitors are free-riding on the technology that was pioneered in the United States.

President Biden tried to restore growth of the Advanced Industries with his three major economic bills; the Infrastucture Investment Act, Chips and Science act, and the Inflation Reduction Act. Whether these economic bills are making a difference in ATI growth or reshoring is too early to tell, but the Trump tariffs, if selectively focused on specific ATI technologies, could make an immediate difference.

The Industrial Commons

As Willy Shih and Gary Pisano argue in their book *Producing Prosperity*,

> "The combination of bad decisions by businesses and inadequate policies by government, has led to an erosion of what we call America's Industrial Commons—the set of manufacturing and technical capabilities that support innovation across a broad range of industries."

I would add that the critical part of the U.S. Industrial Commons, which are seldom mentioned in the press, are the eight NAICS industries shown in Table 5.1. These eight industries are vital because they are part of the Industrial Commons.

As the MNCs moved plants to other countries, they chose to buy many technical services and products like tool and die, foundry, and advanced machining from foreign contractors. The big problem is that as we outsourced products and technologies to foreign countries, we also outsourced the industrial commons. This included the R&D which is best done near the manufacturing process.

We have lost the skills, know-how, and operational competencies, and many of the skilled workers that make up the industrial commons. It is difficult to see how we can achieve a manufacturing renaissance caused by the new tariffs, unless we can rebuild these critical industries and train new skilled workers first.

Declining Federal Research

According to the Information Technology and Innovation Foundation (ITIF), federal basic research has been declining for 22 out of 28 years. As a percentage of GDP, federal research has fallen from a high of 2.5 percent of GDP in 1964 to less than 0.8 percent in 2016.[3] This is a serious red flag, as basic research is the foundation of applied research and fundamental to any innovation strategy.

Basic research expands human knowledge but without easily defined captured commercial benefit. Applied research generates marketable innovation such as improved crop production, treatments for specific diseases, or improved energy efficiency.

Most people do not know that federal basic research was the initial research used in developing the Google search engine, global positioning satellites, supercomputers, artificial intelligence, speech recognition, the Internet, smartphone technologies, the shale gas revolution, seismic imaging, LED light technology, MRI, advanced prosthetics, and the human genome project. Many of these new technologies led to new industries spawning many new markets.

If we want to compete with the Asian and European countries or remain the number one economy in the world, we need to match the research levels of the 1980s which would require an increase of $100 billion per year. There is a high correlation between the investment in basic research and the success of an innovation strategy.

---

[3]Rising Above the Gathering Storm, Revisited. National Academy of Sciences, by members of the 2005 "Rising Above the Gathering Storm" Committee, National Academies Press, Washington D.C., 2010.

The Basic Research Problems

The decline in basic research for university labs is not a new problem. Federal funding for university research and state funding for higher education has been declining for decades. America was once the world leader in government funded research as a percentage of GDP, but has now slipped to twelfth.

There has been a marked interest in funding research that leads to products or patents versus basic research that leads to theoretical knowledge that may, or may not, lead to tangible products and innovations. The problem is that there is no easy way of determining which basic research efforts will directly translate to a new product or technologies.

The development of new technologies into useful products is accomplished by private companies, but many of these products came, initially, from federal basic research in many fields of science. As an example, transistors were not suddenly discovered by the electronics industry; they came from people working with wave mechanics and solid-state physics. Light-emitting diode technology began with the study of infrared emissions from gallium arsenide and other semiconductor alloys. Magnetic resonance imaging came from research into spin echoes and free induction decay.

The disadvantage is that the majority of basic research funding leads to expanding science knowledge not new inventions. So, the gamble is that you must expand the basic research investment to increase the odds of developing a breakthrough inventions.

Another problem is related to Facilities and Administrative (F&A) costs, which are often high and can be perceived as overhead, potentially reducing the amount of funding directly available for research. These costs cover expenses like building upkeep, utilities, administrative staff, and other routine expenses. Universities argue that F&A costs are essential for supporting the infrastructure and administrative processes necessary for conducting research, but critics believe that these are overhead costs that should be covered by the university and are not part of basic research. Many people believe these costs are excessive and should be reduced. Some argue that certain research areas or projects may not be as productive or impactful as others, leading to the perception of waste.

Some also believe that basic research is needlessly complex or impractical, leading to the belief that it is wasteful.

The Trump administration seems to be favoring Milton Friedman who famously argued for abolishing the National Science Foundation, the National Institute of Health and all government funding of higher education (even though his own field received funding). Friedman believed that private sources would fund science, as evidenced by major research that took place before government research funding began. He also believed the efficiency and quality of research would improve when privately funded because government officials' goals divert research from the topics that fit researchers' talent and interests.

Funding basic research is like funding the discovery of a cure for cancer. We spend a lot of money on a wide range of research projects in the hope that some of them will lead to a cure for a specific cancer. It is very expensive research and there are many critics who don't see any payoff. The challenge is from short term investors who want faster return on investments and the new Trump administration who wants to reduce waste in government. Trump has surrounded himself with people who generally believe that government agencies and programs are inefficient and wasteful and should be reduced. The American Institute of Physics reported in July 2024 that House Republicans' appropriations bills for FY 2025 included cuts to federal funding for basic research.

Using America's tripartite approach of government, university labs, and private corporations, basic research did lead to the invention of research breakthroughs like the **computer**, was funded by the military and built by University of Pennsylvania and Harvard; the **transistor**, invented by Bell Labs; the **microprocessor** came from space and strategic missile funding; and the **Internet**, which was conceived by DARPA and built by research universities. These inventions are the foundation for not only the US economy but industries all over the planet.

Basic research is a very expensive way to create innovation and there is no doubt a lot of waste and bureaucracy. It is also undeniable that most of the research leads to new knowledge but not necessarily to new inventions or technologies. Increasingly, corporations seem to value "short-term and incremental innovations, reducible to patents—over the long-term benefits of in-house scientific capabilities."[4] So, the big question and gamble is, can we reduce the basic science research budget and still create the new technologies that will support our strategy of leading the world through innovation; or is the creation of new technologies a function of the size of the basic research budget?

If we are to compete on the world stage with countries like China and our strategy is innovation, we are probably going to have to increase (not cut) the federal budget for basic research to stay in the game. But today the cost cutters and short-term investors are winning the battle of federal budgets and agencies. Who knows where it will lead.

Conclusion

In 2015, President Obama said, "America's future economic growth and international competitiveness depend on our capacity to innovate." His plan, *The Strategy for American Innovation*, also said, innovation-based economic growth will bring greater income, higher quality jobs, and is the key to future prosperity. A strategy of Innovation is a noble idea, but to have a chance, we will need to resolve the following four questions:

1. **Can we increase federal basic research funding?** Advocates of expanding basic research believe that it takes a wide range of research projects, like the US did after World War II, to create the foundation of science that leads to a computer, transistor, or an Internet.

    But today's business climate is not like the post-World War II climate. Today, the US has a trade deficit exceeding 2025 figures - $937 billion trade deficit - $37.6 trillon federal budget deficit - and interest payments on the natioanal debt of $970 billion. Investors want quicker returns and favor applied research over basic research. The U.S. share of the world market for manufactured goods has significantly declined since World War II. Our share fell from 47 percent in 1950 to 17.5 percent in 2022.[5]

---

[4]Scott Andes and Mark Muro, May 28, 2015, U.S. R & D: A troubled enterprise, The Brookings Institute.
[5]Douglas Thomas, January 24, 2020. U.S. Manufacturing Economy, Applied Economics Office, National Institute of Standards, U.S. Department of Commerce.

The trump administration also has the Department of Government Efficiency (DOGE) patrolling federal agencies looking for waste and people to cut and would like to cut the basic research budget another 15 percent. The odds are not in favor of expanding basic research.

2. **How will we reshore the ATIs and specific technologies and reduce their trade deficit?** These industries are absolutely critical to the success of a national innovation strategy, but as of December 2024 the ATI has piled up a $298 billion trade deficit. To reduce the trade deficit there are three alternatives:

   - Consume less and save more—By decreasing consumption and increasing savings, a country's reliance on foreign borrowing is reduced, directly affecting the capital and trade accounts. It seems impractical to ask consumers (many who are living paycheck to paycheck) to reduce their consumption of cheap imported products.

   - Reduce the overvalued dollar—if the value of the dollar can be reduced, a weaker dollar makes imports more expensive and exports cheaper which improves the trade balance.

   - Tax capital inflows—a capital inflow tax like the market access charge (MAC) can reduce the value of the dollar and the trade deficit. Using a **market access charge** for all foreign investors buying U.S. assets would begin to lower the value of the dollar to a trade balancing price.

3. **How do we stop technology from leaving the country** Our foreign competitors use industry subsidies, tariffs, and tax credits to both protect and incentivize their companies to invest. The Biden administration did the same thing with the Chips and Science Act designed to subsidize the industry and offer tax credits to invest in domestic production. The new Trump administration is currently attempting to match the tariffs and trade barriers our foreign competitors have used against us for decades in order to get them to reduce their tariffs and possibly reshore some technologies.

   But there are drawbacks. First, in the current case of trade and federal deficits, I wonder if the United States is in a position to fund more industry subsidies? Second, the tariffs will no doubt inspire retaliatory tariffs from our competitors, with no guarantee that tariffs will lead to reshoring or protecting our technologies.

4. **Some technologies have national security implications—how are we going to protect these technologies?** A report titled "Remaking American Security: *Supply Chain Vulnerabilities & National Security Risks Across the U.S. Defense Industrial Base*" by Brigadier General John Adams found that

> "U.S. national security and the health of the nation's defense industrial base are in jeopardy because of an over-reliance on foreign suppliers for critical defense materials. Foreign sourcing puts America's military readiness in the hands of potentially unreliable or hostile supplier nations and undermines the ability to develop capabilities needed to win on future battlefields."

Protecting specific technologies is a national security issue and the government needs to develop an industrial policy that protects selective industries and technologies. We need to do a lot more to protect the advanced technologies using national security restrictions, and stop or reduce specific technologies from technology transfer agreements with foreign competitors. The Congress also needs to sanction foreign companies who continue to cheat and steal our technology secrets, like they did with the Chinese company Huawei for bank fraud and technology theft. We probably can't do anything about the technologies that are already manufactured in Asia (they already have our secrets), but the government could make up a list of advanced technologies that have national security implications that should not be outsourced.

Perhaps the new Trump tariffs are the first step in developing an industrial policy that can achieve these goals. But the roll-out of Trump's tariff agenda has been haphazard, confusing, and plagued by fits and starts. It would have been very helpful in answering these four questions if tariffs had been introduced as an industrial policy with a plan (like China's 2025 plan) that described priority industries and a list of technologies we want to protect, if we are really going to compete using a strategy of innovation.

My conclusion is that innovation and manufacturing are inextricably linked. If innovation is the strategy that will keep the U.S. economy number one in the world, then the only real hope is to grow the manufacturing sector and protect our technologies.

CHAPTER 8

Critical Minerals and Metal Shortages

The world's sources of critical minerals are increasingly concentrated in just a few countries which leaves the United States and other Western countries very vulnerable to export controls and export bans.

A White House fact sheet of April 12, 2025, said:

Today, President Donald J. Trump declared that foreign trade and economic practices have created a national emergency. Large and persistent annual U.S. goods trade deficits have led to the hollowing out of our manufacturing base; resulted in a lack of incentive to increase advanced domestic manufacturing capacity; undermined critical supply chains; and rendered our defense-industrial base dependent on foreign adversaries.

I would add that outsourcing and the hollowing out of our industrial base, also led to shortages of everything from rare earth minerals and semiconductors to antibiotics and cancer drugs. This scenario makes the United States vulnerable to rogue countries like China who have the power to cut off or restrict imports at any time.

America Has Awakened to Critical Shortages

The COVID-19 crisis was a wake-up call for Americans that showed just how vulnerable globalized supply chains really are. Critical goods like ventilators, masks, and pharmaceuticals were in short supply because of decades of outsourcing which reduced our domestic capacity to manufacture them. An NIH study said, "Throughout the three waves of infection, there were glaring deficiencies in the domestic manufacturing ability to provide necessary supplies."

The COVID-19 emergency woke many people up to the fact that we also have shortages of critical medicines, minerals, metals and components for weapon systems, which have put America into the unenviable position where a foreign competitor could cut off our imports and really harm U.S. industries and consumers. In terms of critical minerals, America is now faced with either reshoring minerals, mining them domestically, or finding other sources.

The following Table 8.1 shows that the United States is 100 percent dependent on foreign countries for 10 critical minerals and 50 to 95 percent dependent on 18 other minerals. It also shows that we are dependent on China for 10 of these critical minerals. China is a source of critical minerals required for a wide range of goods that includes computer chips, robots, electric autos, batteries, drones, and military equipment. It also dominates the refining and processing of many of these critical minerals, including lithium, cobalt, graphite, gallium, rare earth, and many others.

The world's sources of critical minerals are increasingly concentrated in just a few countries which leaves the United States and other Western countries very vulnerable to export controls and export bans. The impact of a "supply shock" can bring higher prices to consumers, production interruptions to manufacturers, stifling a country's ability to find new sources and compete.

Critical Metals and Minerals

Table 8-1 uses data from the U.S. Geological Survey (USGS) to visualize America's import dependence for 30 different key nonfuel minerals along with the nation that exports them to the United States.

Threats and Risks

The Energy Act of 2020 defines a "critical mineral" as a nonfuel mineral or mineral material essential to the economic and national security of the United States, which has a supply chain vulnerable to disruption. Trump has made reducing U.S. dependence on foreign critical minerals a core

Table 8.1 America's import reliance on critical minerals

Critical mineral	Percent reliance	Country
1. Arsenic	100	China—used in semiconductors
2. Fluorspar	100	Mexico—used in cement, steel, aluminum, gasoline, fluorine
3. Gallium	100	China—used for integrated circuits and optical devices like LEDs
4. Graphite	100	China—used for lubricants, batteries, and fuel cells
5. Indium	100	Korea—used as coating of anodes and as a chemical catalyst
6. Manganese	100	Gabon—used in steelmaking and batteries
7. Niobium	100	Brazil—used in steel and super alloys
8. Scandium	100	Europe—rare earth element used for ceramics, alloys, and fuel cells
9. tantalum	100	China—a rare earth element used in capacitors and superalloys
10. yttrium	100	China—used for ceramic, catalysts, lasers, metallurgy, and phosphors
11. Bismuth	95	China—used in medical and atomic research
12. Rare earths	95	China—used in smartphones, electric vehicles, wind turbines and magnets
13. Titanium	95	Japan—used as a white pigment or metal alloys and military aircraft
14. Antimony	83	China— used in lead-acid batteries and flame retardants
15. Chromium	83	S. Africa—used primarily in stainless steel and other alloys
16. Tin	77	Peru—used as protective coatings and alloys for steel
17. Cobalt	76	Congo—used in rechargeable batteries and superalloys
18. Zinc	76	Canada—primarily used in metallurgy to produce galvanized steel
19. Aluminum-bauxite	75	Jamaica—used in more than 500 products
20. Barite	75	China—used in hydrocarbon production
21. Tellurium	75	Canada used in solar cells alloying additive, and thermoelectric devices
22. Platinum	65	S. Africa—used in catalytic converters
23. Nickel	56	Canada—makes stainless steel, superalloys, and rechargeable batteries

(continued)

Table 8.1 America's import reliance on critical minerals (continued)

Critical mineral	Percent reliance	Country
24. Vanadium	54	Canada—primarily used as alloying agent for iron and steel
25. Germanium	50	China—used for fiber optics and night vision applications
26. Magnesium	50	Israel—used as an alloy and for reducing metals
27. Tungsten	50	China—primarily used to make wear-resistant metals
28. Zirconium	50	S. Africa—high-temperature ceramics and corrosion-resistant alloys.
29. Palladium	26	Russia—used in catalytic converters and as a catalyst agent
30 lithium	25	Argentina/Chile?—used for rechargeable batteries

tenet of his national security and economic resilience agenda. So, Trump's aggressive tariff agenda may be asking for a confrontation and retaliation.

China has already demonstrated that they will not hesitate to impose export controls and bans on minerals they control. In 2021, they imposed a ban on exporting graphite to Sweden and to all countries in 2023. In 2023, China banned the export of technology for making rare earth magnets.

China has also put restrictions on seven different kinds of antimony in which the United States is 73 percent dependent on China. Antimony is a flame-retardant metal that is used in making ammunition. The United States has produced 3 million 155 mm shells for the Ukraine war, and restrictions in the supply of antimony could seriously affect our commitment to support Ukraine.

Other countries, such as Russia, could also impose export controls that would impact mineral imports. A 2023 report by the Organisation for Economic Co-operation and Development (OECD) found that Argentina, China, India, Kazakhstan, Russia, and Vietnam imposed the most new export restrictions on critical raw materials from 2009 to 2020. Throughout the Russia–Ukraine war, Russia has imposed export bans on a variety of mineral products, too, including, most recently, precious metal waste and scrap.

According to the World Resources Institute, the U.S. imports rely heavily on foreign sources for rare earth elements, graphite, lithium, and various other metals like manganese, niobium, and tantalum. China controls a significant portion of the processing of these minerals, raising concerns about supply chain security.

Rare Earth Minerals

Rare-earth elements are a group of 17 minerals used in cell phones, magnets, wind turbines, batteries, electric vehicles and military weapon systems. Eighty-five percent of rare earth elements now come from China, which gives them the ability to control supply and paralyze our technology and defense sectors.

The United States used to mine rare earth minerals but the emergence of low-cost suppliers like China and environmental regulations encouraged the United States to rely on foreign suppliers. The United States now imports 91 percent of the rare earth mineral called lanthanum from China. China has 60 to 70 percent of global production and nearly 90 percent of refining capacity. This dominance has positioned China as the undisputed leader in the rare earth market.

The United States has only one operational rare earth mine, and it produces a small fraction of the world's supply. The demand for rare earth minerals is growing due to their use in technologies like semiconductors, camera lenses, lasers, liquid crystal displays, hard disk drives; to name just a few applications.

This increased demand has strained global supplies. This demand, a small number of foreign suppliers, and lack of domestic production has made the United States highly dependent on China and vulnerable because China has used rare earth exports as a tool in trade negotiations. In addition, China and other foreign producers have engaged in wide spread price manipulation, over capacity, and export restrictions to gain economic leverage over the United States which poses a serious national security risk to the U.S. economy and defense preparedness.

On April 15, 2025, President Donald Trump issued an Executive Order (EO) directing the Department of Commerce to investigate under Section 232 of the Trade Expansion Act of 1962, the effects on national security of imports of processed critical minerals and their derivative products, including the prospect of imposing new tariffs. China responded by suspending exports of six heavy rare earth metals, as well as rare earth magnets, in order to "choke off" supplies of components central to automakers, aerospace manufacturers, semiconductor companies and military contractors around the world," the order states.

The investigation will culminate in a report detailing risks and providing recommendations to strengthen domestic production, reduce dependence on foreign suppliers, and enhance economic and national security. Within 180 days, Commerce, in consultation with Secretaries of the Treasury, Defense, and others, were required to report its findings to the President on whether U.S. import reliance on critical minerals and their derivative products threatens national security. The Trump administration has officially determined that the high volume of foreign-sourced critical minerals and metals imports threatens U.S. national security. Citing risks to defense, infrastructure, and technology, the administration has initiated actions, including Section 232 investigations, to reduce reliance on foreign nations—particularly China—and secure supply chains. But, they don't say how they will do it.

The problem is that the United States is 100 percent dependent on foreign countries for 10 critical minerals and 50 to 95 percent dependent on 18 other minerals. So, the question is how can you tariff foreign metals and minerals, when you desperately need them?

The first time China used its rare earth leverage was over a dispute with Japan. China banned the export of rare earth to Japan, which crippled its auto industry for several months. The Japanese ultimately secured a long-term supply from Australia, refined in Malaysia.

China has a global chokehold on rare earth mining and refining. They have worked out a system of export licenses which require end-use disclosure, which effectively gives them a look into all countries and companies usage, end-use products and markets, and where the purchasing country is vulnerable.

The United States and other Western countries are very vulnerable. Whether it is a dispute over Taiwan, the South China sea, or American tariffs, China has the ability to flood specific markets to drive down prices and drive competitors out of business.

Tariffs alone are not going to fix this shortage problem. If the United States is dependent on China for 95 percent of the rare earth used in America today, it is hard to understand how tariffs on the product would help. (Beggars can't be choosers.)

The United States needs a joint coordinated effort, that uses public and private resources to rebuild the rare earth supply chain for not just mining but refining, alternative sources, and research into rare earth alternatives.

The Trump administration has been in negotiations with Ukraine as an alternative source of rare earth but negotiations are stalled because of negotiations on the Russia–Ukraine war. They are also negotiating with Ukraine to secure titanium, used in aircraft wings; lithium, key to several battery technologies; and uranium, used in medical products and weapon systems.

China's rare-earth dominance stems not just from geological luck, but from decades of strategic industrial policy and targeted investment. In contrast, the United States remains fully import-dependent for rare earths and 14 critical minerals and more than 50 percent dependent for another 34. This poses a strategic threat to key sectors, including automotive, semiconductors, defense and clean energy. It also leaves the United States vulnerable to geopolitical pressure in ways that many executives are only now beginning to understand.[1]

Steel and Aluminum

Steel and aluminum are considered vital industries to be protected due to their crucial role in national security, infrastructure, and economic stability. These industries are essential in times of national emergency or conflict like supplying Ukraine in their war with Russia.

Steel and aluminum are fundamental materials for defense-related applications, including military aircraft, ships, vehicles, ammunition, and many other weapons systems. They are also vital for building and maintaining infrastructure, including bridges, buildings, transportation networks, and energy infrastructure. The United States cannot afford to allow these industries to continue to decline or to depend on imports.

The steel and aluminum industries have been declining since the 1970s because of the slow growth of construction in the United States

---

[1]John Jullens, China's Rare-Earth Chokehold, Industry Week, June 20, 2025.

since the 1970s, and the growth of imports. In 2018, the first Trump administration implemented Section 232 tariffs on steel and aluminum. Section 232 allows the president to impose global tariffs and other measures for reasons related to national security.

The Section 232 measures were initially successful and showed that tariffs can work. Major U.S. steel producers like Steel Dynamics, Nucor, and Commercial Metals invested in 15 new steel furnaces and mills, from Florida to Arizona and from West Virginia to Texas. This was a $20 billion investment and created over 4,000 jobs. According to the Coalton for a Prosperous America, American steel workers earned an average of $117,000 per year in 2018.[2]

The 2018 steel and aluminum tariffs have had a mixed record. There was initial recovery in the steel and aluminum industries immediately after the 2018 tariffs, followed by deteriorating economic performance due to widening exemptions and exclusions from the tariffs. The steel and aluminum tariffs of 2018 initially spurred boosts in domestic production, investment, and employment. However, in both cases, those initial boosts were undermined and by some measures reversed by the excessive granting of exclusions by the Trump administration.

The effects were clear: Primary aluminum production slumped, smelters were closed, and employees were laid off. In the steel industry, total steel production has slumped since 2019, and numerous steel mills are being idled and facing closure.

Trump granted exclusions to Mexico and Canada in order to win their approval for a new USMCA agreement. It was a big mistake because Mexico immediately began dumping steel products into the United States by large margins, like rebar (up to 1,700 percent) and hot-dipped galvanized sheet (up 183 percent). Canadian steel and aluminum exports to the United States have increased by 35 percent to $17.7 billion since 2019. It is also inexplicable that the Trump administration also granted South Korea, Brazil, and Argentina significant exemptions, which immediately dampened the effects of the tariffs for U.S. producers. As a result of country exclusions and exemptions, the average effective tariff rate on

[2]CPA Economics Report, Presidential Order to Reinforce Steel/Aluminum, Coalition for a Prosperous America, March 2025.

all steel imports in 2024 was just 3.6 percent. On aluminum, the comparable figure was just 0.8 percent.

On February 10, 2025, President Trump signed proclamations to close existing loopholes and exemptions and restore a true 25 percent tariff on steel and elevate the tariff to 25 percent on aluminum. The order says, "Key reforms include eliminating all alternative agreements, applying strict "melted and poured" standards, expanding tariffs to include key downstream products, terminating all general approved exclusions, and cracking down on tariff misclassification and duty evasion schemes.

In June 2025, President Trump raised the tariff on steel and aluminum imports from 25 percent to 50 percent. Tariffs on steel and aluminum imports from the UK would remain at 25 percent, with possible changes or quotas, depending on the status of the U.S.–UK Economic Prosperity Deal. The steel and aluminum tariffs will apply only to the steel and aluminum contents of imported products, whereas the nonsteel and nonaluminum contents of imported products will be subject to other applicable tariffs.

Trump created the steel and aluminum tariff problem because of his making special deals on exclusions and exemptions. Let's hope that Trump won't compromise the tariffs with more political wrangling.

Aluminum

In 2000, the United States had 23 domestic smelters. In 2018, when Trump issued his first tariffs the United States their number had declined to seven. In 2025, the number is down to four smelters. The big question is, will the United States allow the last four smelters to close and be 100 percent dependent on imports?

Aluminum is a versatile metal used in a vast array of products. It's estimated that over 500 major products utilize aluminum. This includes everything from beverage cans and kitchen utensils to aircraft, buildings, and electronics. In February 2025, the Trump administration announced 25 percent tariffs on all steel and aluminum products. But tariffs alone will probably not reverse the 25-year decline in domestic production of aluminum.

The demand for aluminum will only grow, and grow faster, as the U.S. economy transitions to mass adoption of clean energy systems—nearly all of which require increasing amounts of aluminum.

The main obstacle to a U.S. aluminum resurgence is the cost of energy. Electricity costs are 40 percent of production costs. The amount of electricity to produce aluminum exceeds that for any other comparable material. And the price of electricity across the country spiked after the Russian invasion of Ukraine and remains high. Energy costs were the main factor leading to the last plant closure. Canada's aluminum smelters have significantly lower energy costs than their U.S. counterparts. Thanks to abundant, low-cost hydroelectric power, Canadian smelters enjoy energy costs up to three times lower than their U.S. counterparts.

The aluminum industry will be competing with other industries such as the hundreds of $billions invested in data centers all over the United States. The Trump tariff of 50 percent won't be enough to grow the aluminum industry. It will probably take an investment in both clean energy and nuclear plants to satisfy future industry energy needs.

But energy costs are not the only threat to the aluminum industry. The U.S. Department of Commerce recently found that 14 different countries were dumping aluminum extrusion products (www.trade.gov/preliminary-determinations-ad-investigations-aluminum-extrusions-multiple-countries) into the United States at below-market value. These countries include China, Colombia, Ecuador, India, Indonesia, Italy, Malaysia, Mexico, South Korea, Taiwan, Thailand, Turkey, the United Arab Emirates, and Vietnam. Commerce found that these countries were exporting subsidized or artificially low-priced aluminum extrusions, flooding markets worldwide, and unfairly undercutting domestic U.S. producers.

The United States currently imports roughly half, or about 47 percent, of the aluminum consumed in the United States. Canada is the largest single supplier of aluminum to the United States, according to S&P Global Market Intelligence data. In 2024, the U.S. imported about 4.8 million metric tons of aluminum.

The top four countries supplying aluminum to the United States in 2024 were the following: Canada: $11.47 billion (40.68 percent); China: $3.07 billion (10.85 percent); Mexico: $1.84 billion (6.53 percent); United Arab Emirates: $1.28 billion (4.50 percent).

Conclusion

Before researching this chapter, I must admit that I knew there were serious shortages, but I did not know that they were so extensive and such a threat to our economy and national security. I will go so far as to say I don't think America has a choice but to take action to relieve many of the shortages in the near future. I would add, that if some of the solutions are to reshore products, find new sources for critical minerals or medicines, or to reduce imports, I don't think that we will have the leverage to do it unless we use tariffs, subsidies, tax incentives, and monetary pressure.

The multinational corporations who have been outsourcing many of the products and materials described in this chapter, were responsible for getting America into this mess. I call the multinationals four decades of outsourcing "cutting a prime cut out of the carcass of the American economy." They did it for short-term profits and shareholder value in a manner that can only be described by one word—greed. They went for the money and ignored the future, and the U.S. government supported them.

The dilemma is that it may be in the DNA of capitalism to always pursue low costs and short-term profits, regardless of the potential future losses and long-term problems. The short-term strategies and aggressive outsourcing got America into the current shortage jam and it will take a long time, a lot of investment, and government subsidies to get us out.

Because of these shortages, The United States is now in a very weak position that has made it vulnerable to predatory economic pricing, market manipulation strategies, and extortion. A good example is the copper industry. According to the United States Geological Survey (USGS), the United States relies on imports of roughly 45 to 46 percent of consumed copper. At the same time China has been building up massive subsidized overcapacity in copper smelting and refining now approaching 50 percent of global output. This allows China to manipulate prices and drive foreign competitors out of business.

Trump responded on July 30 using Section 232 of the trade expansion act to impose tariffs on semi-finished copper and copper derivative products. China is responding to the U.S. tariffs by transshipping copper products through countries like Vietnam. China also has invested in copper plants in the United States and some draw taxpayer subsidies. Tariff evasion, subsidies, and dumping are all part of the China strategy to dominate the copper industry, and the United States is not in a good position to stop them.

The country and many of its industries and manufacturers will suffer unless we can find ways to reduce the shortages, reshore some of the products and materials, or find new sources that are dependable and allied.

So, What Can We Do?

1. **Investing in domestic manufacturing of minerals and metals**—A model already exists for government assistance to do this. It is the Chips and Science Act. The CHIPS and Science Act aims to revitalize the U.S. semiconductor industry by incentivizing domestic manufacturing and research and development. It allocated $52.7 billion in funding. It aims to strengthen the domestic supply chain and reduce reliance on foreign chip manufacturing.

   Results—The Commerce Department has announced over $30 billion in proposed CHIPS private sector investments spanning 23 projects in 15 states. These projects include 16 new semiconductor manufacturing facilities and are expected to create over 115,000 manufacturing and construction jobs across the country.

   Before we can apply this government subsidy model to the critical minerals industries, the government needs to select and prioritize the most important minerals and industries. This assumes that the Congress will be sympathetic and fund the project. After the budget exercise of mid-2025 and the DOGE efforts at cutting federal agency budgets and programs, funding another Chips Act type project doesn't look very probable unless Congress views the shortages as a true national security threat.

2. **Tariffs**—I believe that tariffs could be used to incentivize many American corporations to reshore production, provide an incentive for foreign competitors to reduce export restrictions and

price manipulation, and to reduce critical mineral shortages. But the Trump tariffs have not been based on a comprehensive plan, or industry and product priorities. Trump continually changes his mind and his tariff announcements are an on again off again program that uses a broad axe approach. Another problem is the question of how can you use a tariff against a country who has mineral or materials you absolutely need in your industries without making exemptions?

3. **Increase strategic stockpiles**—According to Reuters (August 21, 2023), China is way ahead of the United States and is stockpiling aluminum ingots, cobalt, copper, indium, molybdenum, nickel, rare earth elements, tungsten, and refined zinc.

   America also has a stockpile called the National Defense Stockpile but it doesn't include critical minerals like lithium, cobalt, rare earth elements (REEs), and certain battery-grade nickel. Congress has allocated funds for stockpiling and strengthening domestic mineral production. The Defense Production Act has allocated around $700 million for critical minerals, including $19 million for a tin smelting and a refining facility in Pennsylvania and $37.5 million for graphite development in Alaska. The Department of Defense has awarded over $439 million since 2020 to establish domestic rare earth element supply chains, including for cobalt, graphite, and tungsten. But minerals like bismuth, and fluorspar, the metals copper, and lead despite being used by the military, are not currently stockpiled. To be a solution for critical mineral shortages the U.S. stockpile needs to be expanded.

4. **Finding alternative suppliers**—The USGS, through Earth MRI and other programs, is exploring new sites for critical minerals, including those in Wyoming and Montana. This includes researching the potential of mine waste as a source of these minerals, and offering funding to states to evaluate mine waste. The government is also collaborating with allies like Canada, Australia, and the UK to secure supplies of key minerals, including cobalt, graphite, and tungsten.

5. **Recycling**—The DOE is promoting recycling and repurposing of materials to extend their lifespan and reduce the need for virgin material extraction. Recycling old minerals and tailings involves

various steps, including efficient ore processing, selective mining, recycling and reuse of waste materials, and advanced technologies like flotation and bioleaching. It also includes repurposing materials like slag and tailings in construction, road building, or backfilling operation. While the potential for recovering valuable materials exists, the economic feasibility is uncertain and varies depending on factors like mineral prices, extraction costs, and environmental regulations.

To incentivize private sector investment in recycling, the government will probably have to issue: tax credits and subsidies. These can help offset the costs of setting up and operating recycling facilities, encouraging private companies to invest in this sector.

The government will also have to create a stable and predictable regulatory environment to build confidence among investors, encouraging them to commit to long-term projects, and reduce the time and cost associated with obtaining the necessary approvals for recycling projects. The government will also have to fund training programs to prepare workers for jobs in the recycling industry, says the IEA.

Perhaps the biggest hurdle for implementing these strategies, will be the Environmental Protection Agency. Opening up old toxic mines and recycling materials will require a modification of many regulations if we are going to have a chance of creating an economically viable and sustainable mineral and recycling industry.

6. **Reopening old mines**—The United States has 140,000 abandoned hard rock mines, potentially holding a variety of critical minerals. While the exact number of critical minerals in these closed mines is unknown, many of the 50 minerals deemed critical by the USGS are likely to be present. Examples include cobalt, lithium, nickel, manganese, and rare earth elements.

Many of these old mines were closed because of toxicity problems which will require overcoming environmental challenges and regulatory hurdles. This includes ensuring that extraction and processing are environmentally friendly and sustainable. Also, new technologies are enabling the recovery of minerals from legacy wastes and e-waste. For example, bioleaching, ligand-based extraction and separation, and electrochemical separation are making it possible to extract valuable minerals from otherwise unusable materials. Reopening mines will require governments to provide incentives for investment, streamlining permitting processes, and working with the mining industry.

There is legislation related to reopening and managing abandoned mineral mines in the United States called the "Good Samaritan Remediation of Abandoned Hardrock Mines Act," signed into law in December 2024, which creates a pilot program to allow for low-risk cleanups of abandoned hard rock mines. Additionally, there are regulations regarding reopening mines under the authority of the Mine Safety and Health Administration (MSHA), and other legislation aims to modernize mining laws and address the environmental impacts of mining.

7. **The danger of unstable countries: Democratic Republic of Congo**—Eighty percent of the world's cobalt is in the Democratic Republic of the Congo (DRC). The United States uses cobalt in a wide variety of products from rechargeable batteries and superalloys to hard metals, magnets, and medical implants. Rwanda is heavily suspected in supporting the M23 rebels, who are fighting against the Congolese government in the eastern Congo. It has created a zone of instability and violence that jeopardizes cobalt mining operations and worker safety. Mining is also linked to human rights abuses and child labor violations. Seventy-six percent of our raw cobalt ore comes from the Congo, but it is refined by countries like Norway and Canada. The situation is even more complicated by the fact that Chinese companies either own or operate around 80 percent of the total cobalt output from the DRC. Suffice it to say, that our dependence on countries like the DRC is a high-risk venture, but if we are to seek alternative sources around the world, it is a game we must play.

CHAPTER 9

Pharmaceutical Shortages

We have surrendered control of our medicine supply to China and India—and patients are paying the price

The growing U.S. dependence on China and India for widely used generic pharmaceuticals creates serious risks to national security and patient safety. China now accounts for 95 percent of imports of ibuprofen, 91 percent of imports of hydrocortisone, 70 percent of imports of acetaminophen (Tylenol), and 40 to 45 percent of imports of penicillin. The United States is dependent on imports for two-thirds of generic medicines, which are 90 percent of all prescriptions. America is dangerously dependent on drugs from India and China and any restrictions of their shipments would be a disaster for hospitals and clinics.

The drug shortage crisis is the result of decades of offshoring American drug manufacturing capacity, failures of the U.S. Food and Drug Administration (FDA) to regulate and oversee foreign drug manufacturers, and the U.S. government doing nothing about the offshoring of critical medicines for decades. Foreign governments also used massive subsidies to artificially lower prices, making it impossible for American manufacturers to compete.

The big threat is that any political problems, export restrictions, or factory disruptions in these exporting countries could lead to many more drug shortages and immediate problems for clinics, doctors and patients. The following 10-year trend chart shows that the United States already has serious shortages, and they will probably get much worse as China and India retaliate for Trumps tariffs.

Figure 9.1 shows a 10-year trend indicating that the United States has already a severe shortage problem, reaching a high of 309 drug shortages in 2023. Some of the most damaging shortages are in generic cancer

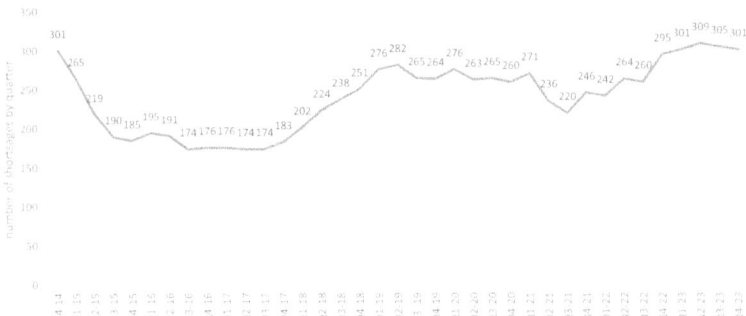

*Figure 9.1 The number of drug shortages in the United States over
a 10-year period*

Source: American Society of Health System Pharmacists. Gunes, approved by Michael Ganio
on November 7, 2025. https://news.asdhp.org/news/meetingnews/2024/12/11/executive/view

drugs used for many kinds of cancers. A study[1] in 2023 by the American
Cancer Society found that one in ten patients have suffered from drug
shortages. One cancer patient wrote this in reply to the survey: "My doc-
tor office only gets enough for one patient a month. I'm currently set to
get mine in over six months."

Last year, the FDA allowed the cancer drug cisplatin to be sold in the
United States from an uninspected lab in China. Faced with shortages
and a limited number of suppliers, almost all of them overseas, the FDA
is being forced to relax its standards, just to find any supplier of certain
badly needed drugs. Beggars can't be choosers.

Critical Drug Shortage Examples

Statin Drug Atorvastatin. It is a drug for cardiovascular disease and is
used by millions of people. Atorvastatin is available from nine different
drugmakers, including companies based in Germany, Bangladesh and
Turkey, and all of these companies depend on one Indian company, Ind-
Swift Laboratories Ltd, for the active pharmaceutical ingredients (APIs)
to make atorvastatin. And Ind-Swift depends on five Chinese companies
for the key starting materials (KSMs) to make the APIs. So, the entire

---

[1]Survivor Views: Drug Shortages, Telehealth, and Biomarker Testing, The
American Cancer Society, September 2023.

supply chain for this drug depends on China. And there are shortages of Atorvastatin now reported in the United States, the UK, and Canada. It is a daisy chain supply chain that goes back to China.

Antibiotic Benzathine Penicillin. Its production is entirely dependent on three Chinese API manufacturers. The shortage is said to be due to a combination of manufacturing constraints and unexpectedly increased demand. It is badly needed in the United States because of an outbreak of syphilis.

Antibiotic Amoxicillin—Another antibiotic medication used to treat a variety of bacterial infections is amoxicillin. which is a type of penicillin. There is only one remaining U.S. facility producing amoxicillin in Bristol, Tennessee to treat the entire country. But now the plant is struggling to keep its doors open even as the United States struggles with an amoxicillin shortage crisis.

Blood Thinner Heparin—It is a lifesaving blood thinner and one of the five most-used therapeutics. Heparin comes from Chinese pigs. The FDA once considered cattle-based heparin but shifted away in the 1990s due to worries over "mad cow" disease. In 2016, the FDA acknowledged that cattle-based heparin is a workable alternative and is encouraging its reintroduction. China is a significant exporter of heparin, with a large portion of the world's heparin supply originating from there.

The top five drug classes behind the current spate of shortages are, in order, central nervous system (CNS) drugs, antimicrobials, hormone agents, chemotherapies and fluids, and electrolytes, according to ASHP (American Society of Health System Pharmacists.) Forty-six percent of the drug shortages in the first quarter of 2024 were injectables.

In 2024, the United States imported $212 billion in pharmaceutical products and had a trade deficit of $127 billion in medicinal and pharmaceutical products. The FDA lists 153 drugs that are currently on shortage lists, which leaves U.S. hospitals, pharmacies, and patients dependent on unstable and undependable foreign supply chains. According to the Coaltion for a Prosperous America (CPA), there are 100 drugs prescribed in the U.S. whose supply is dependent on a single factory in China.

A recent medical study demonstrated that patients taking generic drugs produced in India were 54 percent more likely to experience serious adverse events than those taking equivalent U.S.-manufactured generics.[2] FDA investigations also uncovered criminal violations of Good Manufacturing Practices at Indian pharmaceutical plants, including falsified safety data and dangerous contamination issues. Similarly, China has a troubling history of safety scandals, notably the deadly 2008 heparin contamination that killed dozens of Americans.

Conclusion

Early in the COVID-19 pandemic, a global shortage of hospital gowns, gloves, surgical masks, and respirators caused policymakers globally to panic. China increased imports and decreased exports of this personal protective equipment, removing supplies from world markets. It revealed to US citizens that we lost control of these vital medical items, and left ourselves at the mercy of China, who decreased exports to protect its own health care industry.

China has already demonstrated its willingness to use economic leverage on products we depend on. If hostilities between the United States and China continue to rise or if China invades Taiwan, we would be at grave risk of seeing vital pharmaceutical supplies reduced or cut off entirely.

These shortages reveal how the current U.S. trade system and outsourcing has failed to ensure a stable medicine supply—while devastating the domestic producers who once sustained it. Once outsourcing of pharmaceuticals began, foreign countries like China and India saw an opportunity to gain market dominance. Government subsidies enabled them to undercut U.S. producers with low prices which caused many plant closures and bankruptcies in the United States. As a result, imports began to hollow out America's pharmaceutical base. In 2002, U.S. manufacturers produced 84 percent of domestically consumed pharmaceuticals. In 2023, the number declined to 37 percent of the domestic market.

The collapse of U.S. pharmaceutical manufacturing is the result of decades of free trade, increased market penetration due to state-sponsored

---

[2]Jeff Grabmeier, All generic drugs are not equal, Generics made in India have more "severe adverse events" study finds, Ohio State News, February 19, 2025.

subsidies and dumping, and the absence of government protection or and industry strategy. According to the CPA,

> This is not a supply chain problem. This is a trade and industrial policy failure. We have built the market in which essential medicines are priced so low that no one wants to make them. Then we express shock when they disappear from the shelf and patients lose treatment. The dangerous consequences of offshoring our pharmaceutical base are already here—ration care, patient delays, and empty shelves. We have surrendered control of our medicine supply to China and India—and patients are paying the price.[3]

I would add that perhaps it is in the DNA of capitalism to pursue low prices around the world despite long-term problems to our economy and citizens. In this case the only protection is from the government by developing a long-term industrial plan with specific policies to counter foreign country cheating and incentives for reshoring and domestic protection.

Solutions

Today we are as helpless as a hog on a turnspit and one wonders how and why the government allowed the American health care system to get into this dependency with the resulting shortages. There are two major problems. First, outsourcing has led to shortages, quality and safety problems. Second. outsourcing to the lowest cost producers in Asia did not lead to low prices for consumers because of wholesalers, distributors, and pharmacy benefit managers (PBMs) who add layers of costs contributing to inflated prices. The government needs to take immediate action to reduce import dependency, particularly from adversarial nations, and offer incentives to expand domestic manufacturing.

This is what has happened so far:

- On April 1, 2025, the U.S. Department of Commerce initiated a Section 232 investigation under the Trade Expansion Act of 1962

---

[3]Andrew Rechenberg, America's Drug Shortage Isn't a Supply Problem—It's a Production, Coalition for a Prosperous America, June 16, 2025.

to determine the effects on national security of imports of pharmaceuticals and pharmaceutical ingredients, including "finished drug products, medical countermeasures, critical inputs such as active pharmaceutical ingredients, key starting materials, and derivative products of those items." The investigation confirms that the United States has extreme overreliance on foreign pharmaceutical supplies—especially active pharmaceutical ingredients (APIs) and critical injectable drugs from China and India. The investigation concludes that this dependence is a threat to U.S. national security and patient safety. President Trump and Secretary of Commerce Howard Lutnick have said the intent of the investigations is to enable the imposition of tariffs.

The investigation also says that

The United States has less than five percent of the world's population and yet funds around three quarters of global pharmaceutical profits. This egregious imbalance is orchestrated through a purposeful scheme in which drug manufacturers deeply discount their products to access foreign markets, and subsidize that decrease through enormously high prices in the United States.

Drug manufacturers, rather than seeking to equalize evident price discrimination, agree to other countries demands for low prices, and simultaneously fight against the ability for public and private payers in the United States to negotiate the best prices for patients. The inflated prices in the United States fuel global innovation while foreign health systems get a free ride.

The Section 232 order says,

This abuse of Americans' generosity, who deserve low-cost pharmaceuticals on the same terms as other developed nations, must end. Americans will no longer be forced to pay almost three times more for the exact same medicines, often made in the exact same factories. As the largest purchaser of pharmaceuticals, Americans should get the best deal.

President Trump goes on to say:

> "Americans must therefore have access to the most-favored-nation price for these products. My Administration will take immediate steps to end global freeloading and, should drug manufacturers fail to offer American consumers the most-favored-nation lowest price, my Administration will take additional aggressive action."

Section 4 is titled Enabling Direct-to-Consumer Sales to American Patients at the Most-Favored-Nation Price and states that "To the extent consistent with law, the Secretary of Health and Human Services (Secretary) shall facilitate direct-to-consumer purchasing programs for pharmaceutical manufacturers that sell their products to American patients at the most-favored-nation price."

Administering tariffs and quotas will be tricky. As pointed out earlier, China has the leverage and power to restrict or cut off many minerals, and materials needed by the United States and will retaliate against trump's tariffs and quotas. Hopefully the Trump administration will implement tariffs on specific products and industries, and leave the door open for negotiation with China to insure we don't shoot ourselves in the foot. But if we don't find a way to monetarily punish China and India, the old adage, "Mercy to the wolf is cruelty to the lambs," will apply.

There is legislation in Congress called the Producing Incentives for Long-term Production of Lifesaving Supply of Medicines Act, known as the PILLS Act, which would provide corporate tax credits for pharmaceutical companies to invest in U.S.-based manufacturing facilities. The bill was introduced by Rep. Claudia Tenney (R-NY). The bill uses the tax credit techniques of the Inflation Reduction Act to stimulate U.S. companies to invest in the production of APIs and finished doses of generic medicines in either pill or injectable form. Even though the bill has been supported by both Democrats and Republicans it is debated at a time when Republicans are trying to find more costs to cut in the 2025 budget.

It is interesting to note that the pharmaceutical companies that rushed to outsource their drugs to the low-cost countries and created this problem, now are asking the government to offer tax incentives and low-cost loans to reshore their production—just like the semiconductor industry did in the Chips Act.

It is now obvious that the FDA has been ineffective at managing America's generic drug shortage, drug quality, or drug safety problems. They know which foreign labs have had safety and quality problems but have not been able to regulate them, primarily due to resource limitations and the complex nature of global drug supply chains. While the FDA has authority to inspect foreign facilities, it says it doesn't have the resources to inspect every facility, particularly with the growing number of overseas manufacturers.

Providing the needed resources will be up to Congress, which has not been very sympathetic to the FDA problems and has eliminated 3,500 FDA jobs as part of a larger workforce reduction within the Department of Health and Human Services (HHS), and is still searching for more costs to cut in federal agencies. The 2026 budget also includes a 3.6%, $271 million further cut to the FDA.

This example demonstrates the foolishness of across-the-board budget reductions that do not examine the individual needs or objectives of an agency. It is throwing the baby out with the bathwater. It is not likely that we will make progress on the drug quality or safety problems in the near future if Congress continues to cut FDA resources.

Another solution would be for Congress to establish strategic stockpiles of critical drugs and minerals to safeguard against shock or short-term disruptions. This would also have to be approved by Congress and run the risk of cuts in the latest struggle with budget cuts. If the stockpiling of critical drugs is approved. the next step would be to allow shipments into our country tariff free, which might be politically difficult unless Trump approves exemptions on specific classes of drugs.

Outsourcing drug production to lower-cost Asian producers **did not** lead to lower drug prices for consumers due to several factors, including:

1. International studies show that U.S. drug prices are significantly higher than those in other countries. Many countries have single-payer systems or centralized negotiation, allowing them to bargain for lower prices, while the U.S. system lacks a central

negotiator and relies on individual health plans, reducing their bargaining power.

2. Unlike other countries, the United States doesn't have price controls or limits on how much pharmaceutical companies can charge for drugs.

3. The U.S. health care system is fragmented, with thousands of health plans negotiating with drug manufacturers, weakening the overall bargaining power.

4. Pharmaceutical companies can extend patent lifespans through various tactics, delaying generic competition and keeping prices high for longer periods.

5. The complexity of the U.S. drug supply chain and lack of transparency allow for profit maximization at various stages.

6. The United States doesn't use value-based pricing, where drug prices are tied to the actual value they provide, allowing for high prices regardless of clinical benefits.

7. Drug companies agree to confidential rebates with foreign customers, and countries who use tiered pricing, which can lead to high prices in middle-income markets.

8. Tariffs on imported drugs and APIs can increase the cost of imports, potentially offsetting the savings from outsourcing.

CHAPTER 10

Semiconductors, Auto Parts, Rechargeable Batteries, Solar Panels, Aviation Components, and Magnets

Losing control of the supply of many critical products has made us susceptible to price manipulation and economic extortion.

Critical minerals and pharmaceutical shortages are vital to the economy and dominate the headlines. However, it is not well known that there are many other industries and products from semiconductors to solar panels that are also facing shortages.

Automobile Parts

The auto parts industry has lost 341 establishments and 168,003 employees since 2002. According to the Automotive Aftermarket Network, the United States imported $197.3 billion of auto parts in 2024. In the same year the United States exported $82.8 billion of auto parts for a $114.5 billion trade deficit.

Foreign auto manufacturers who have plants in the United States import most of their parts from their country, rather than buying locally from U.S. manufacturers. In addition, automakers have moved toward a more integrated North American production model, with parts being sourced from Canada and Mexico to be assembled in the U.S. They also buy parts from China. Free trade agreements like the USMCA (formerly NAFTA) have also facilitated the flow of goods and parts across borders, influencing where parts are manufactured and imported.

The U.S. auto industry is closely intertwined with global auto supply chains, with parts often crossing borders multiple times before reaching the final assembly line. The Trump tariffs have impacted the cost and availability of imported auto parts, potentially increasing the cost of manufacturing in the United States. Whether the tariffs will reduce the importation of foreign auto parts or increase reshoring of auto parts production and jobs is still an open question.

Batteries

The United States is lagging behind China and the European Union in the production of lithium-ion batteries for electric vehicles because of limited access to the critical materials used in battery components (see Chapter 8). There are some significant investments in new battery plants because of the Inflation Reduction Act, but if the United States wants to control its supply chain, the government is going to have to develop better domestic sources of rare earth materials and lithium. Battery storage also uses cobalt, graphite, and manganese. The United States is 100 percent dependent on imports for graphite and manganese. In 2024, we were also 76 percent dependent on imports of cobalt and approximately 50 percent of lithium. If we can't find better sources for these minerals then building more battery plants in the United States becomes an academic exercise.

Rechargeable Batteries

The commercialization of rechargeable batteries has moved offshore along with new innovation capacity. The United States struggles to become self-sufficient in rechargeable battery production due to a reliance on foreign suppliers, not controlling critical minerals, and the high cost of developing domestic mining operations. Additionally, the United States lacks the manufacturing expertise and logistics infrastructure that exists in other regions.

Although the original invention of the Lithium-ion (Li-ion) battery took place in U.S. laboratories housed in U.S. universities, and funded by the federal government, the United States is now at a competitive disadvantage, relying on foreign suppliers for both current products and next generation batteries. Lithium-ion (Li-ion) batteries are built on complex chemistries that offer superior weight savings per unit of energy density. They last a long time during disuse and are low-maintenance. To have a chance of increasing the manufacture of rechargeable batteries in the United States, we will first have to solve the mineral shortage problem described in chapter 8.

Solar Panels

Solar panels use arsenic, germanium, indium, and tellurium. The United States is highly dependent on imports of these four minerals, with some being entirely import-reliant. Arsenic is 100 percent import-reliant, having no domestic production since 1985. Germanium is also significantly import-reliant, with the United States relying on foreign sources for over 50 percent. Indium is 100 percent import-reliant, and tellurium relies on foreign sources for more than 75 percent.

Our biggest competitor for solar panels is China who has 80 percent of the global production at all stages. This dominance extends to various stages of the manufacturing process, including polysilicon, ingots, wafers, and cells. Several reports and investigations suggest that China's solar panel factories produce significantly more solar panels than the global market demands, leading to an oversupply.

China's government provides subsidies to its solar panel manufacturers, enabling them to sell products at prices below the cost of production in foreign markets, which is referred to as "dumping." Dumping allows Chinese companies to gain market share in foreign markets. Investigations by the U.S. Commerce Department have found that some Chinese companies have bypassed U.S. trade laws and tariffs by exporting solar panels through Southeast Asian countries to be exported to the United States. These problems could be reduced if Trump tariffs on China stay in place and the United States also tariffs the transshipping countries such as Mexico, Thailand, and Vietnam.

Based on 2025 reports, the removal of federal tax credits for electric vehicles (EVs) and solar panels, along with the imposition of new tariffs, is expected to significantly reduce demand, slow down industry adoption, and disrupt domestic manufacturing expansion.

Aviation Components

Building commercial and military airplanes requires the use of niobium, tantalum, vanadium to enhance strength, durability, and high-temperature resistance. They are incorporated into superalloys and other critical components like turbine blades and jet engines. These metals enable the construction of lighter yet stronger structures, as well as components that can withstand the extreme heat and stress generated during flight.

The United States is 100 percent dependent on imports for niobium, tantalum, and vanadium and tantalum comes from China. While the United States does produce some vanadium, it is still 50 percent import-reliant to meet U.S. aviation demand.

Magnets

High-tech magnets, particularly rare earth magnets like neodymium magnets, are used extensively in manufacturing across many industries and are used to produce almost every modern convenience today. They power everything from electric motors in hybrid and electric vehicles to small but powerful devices like smartphones and hard drives. They are used in:

1. Automotive Industry: Electric Motors, Electric Vehicles, Sensors, and Alternators:
2. Electronics: Speakers and Microphones: Hard Drives, Smartphone Miniaturization.
3. Other Industries: Wind Turbines, Industrial Machinery, MRI scanners and other medical devices, recycling, permanent magnets.
4. Military applications including precision-guided munitions, tank navigation systems, and electronic countermeasures equipment.

Even though American research initially developed this important technology, production of high-tech magnets has migrated offshore. Today, there is no domestic neodymium–iron–boron (NdFeB) magnet producer, and 75 percent of NdFeB magnets are fabricated in China. The disappearance of a U.S. magnet industry has eroded U.S. leadership in patents and our ability to design new applications.

Semiconductors

After decades of outsourcing, today only 12 percent of semiconductors are manufactured in the United States. Semiconductors are like the aluminum industry in that they are used in hundreds of products including: smartphones, aircraft, autos, weapons systems, electronics, and the electric grid to name just a few. As a result, they are critical to U.S. economic and national security.

Both the industry and the government ignored the outsourcing problem until a semiconductor shortage led to disruptions in the U.S. auto industry. Semiconductor supply chain disruptions were due to shortages of critical minerals like lithium and cobalt, leading to fewer cars available for purchase.

These industries have finally realized that they had no control of deliveries and were going to be faced with shortages from now on.

National Security and Defense

The Department of Defense, has put many military weapon systems in jeopardy because of their ongoing purchasing of components that use 12 foreign minerals deemed critical for national and defense purposes, including antimony, arsenic, bismuth, gallium, germanium, indium, natural graphite, rare earth elements, scandium, tantalum, tungsten, and yttrium. The United States imports 100 percent of these critical minerals and metals used in military systems and components, and is heavily reliant on imports for many others. For example, the United States is 100 percent reliant on imports for natural graphite and gallium, and heavily relies on imports for rare earth elements, nickel, cobalt, and lithium. This dependence creates vulnerabilities, and supply chain disruption that can hinder production, maintenance, and modernization of military equipment.

These critical minerals and metals are essential components in various military systems, including weapon systems, aircraft, and electronic equipment. For instance, chromium is used in steel alloys for armor and other structural components. Gallium is a key component in semiconductors, which are vital for missile guidance systems and advanced computers. The CIA reports that the United States is 83 percent import-reliant for chromium and 100 percent import-reliant for gallium. If the supply of these minerals is disrupted, it can negatively impact military readiness. For chromium, the United States relies heavily on imports, with South Africa being a primary source for chromite (ores and concentrates). While the United States has imported scandium in the past, primarily from countries like China and Russia, it is now 100 percent import dependent.

As described in Chapter 8, these shortages highlight the need for finding alternative sources, increasing domestic production and mining, and using selective tariffs if we want to ensure national security

Conclusion—Reducing Shortages and Regaining Control over Imports

Chapters 8 to 10 described how shortages have put America into the unenviable position of losing control of the supply of many critical products and materials thus making us susceptible to price manipulation and economic extortion. They have also made citizens vulnerable as in the case of life sustaining medicines.

If a country like China, should decide to suddenly stop all export to America for political reasons, the United States would be trapped in a situation of our own making where we could not in the short run come up with an alternative supply. In the case of critical minerals, manufacturing operations would come to a halt. In the case of critical medicine like cancer drugs, people would die. The government does not yet have a strategic plan that offers solutions to export bans on critical products and materials.

To do this we must reclaim supply chains from China and other countries for everything from pharmaceuticals to semiconductors. I don't think it is possible without some kind of monetary pressure on:

- U.S. companies to reshore products
- Foreign countries to reduce exports to the United States, running surpluses, manipulating currencies and dumping products into the United States below their production costs
- The government to help find new sources of products that can't be sourced from the United States

The Reshoring paradox—One of the problems of reshoring is the investment cost to make it again in the United States and whether the highly skilled labor is available or must be trained from scratch. Another factor is the time it would take to reshore a product like iPhones.

Apple estimates that it would take many years and cost billions of dollars to build new plants and production lines to manufacture iPhones in the United States. They also estimated that the retail price would increase anywhere from $1,500 to $3,500 per phone. In addition, Apple CEO Tim Cook does not think there is a labor pool with enough workers with the vocational skills to manufacture iPhones in the United States. Apple makes a good point in that some outsourced products, particularly consumer products, may not have a justification for reshoring. It also makes the case to first develop a list of the most critical products in an order of priority.

I believe that to have a chance of coming up with legislation that will positively help any of these shortage problems will require the Congress to overcome its current polarized state. It will only happen if both parties can work in a bipartisan manner and work together on solutions to very complicated problems. Albert Schweitzer said, "The time will come when pessimism and optimistic thought, which hitherto talked past each other almost as strangers, will have to meet for practical discussion." That time has come and we either have a practical discussion or accept shortages as our future.

China has a strategic advantage over the United States because they developed a 10-year plan called Made in China 2025 that listed and prioritized the industries and technologies they wanted to dominate. Free market critics of industrial policy in the United States argue that government officials lack the needed information and expertise to devise such a plan. They don't like the idea of the government picking winners and losers in the economy. They also fear that subsidies and other interventions can lead to inefficiencies, protect uncompetitive industries, and ultimately harm overall economic growth. So free traders and globalists got their way and we now have declining industries and critical shortages without a plan except for executive orders and tariffs. It is all part of the globalization trap.

CHAPTER 11

Dollar Value and the Financialization of the Economy

The question of tariffs has resulted in a titanic struggle between the financial sector that wants a strong dollar and status quo, and those who want to grow domestic manufacturing.

For decades administrations, both Democrat and Republican, endorsed a free trade orthodoxy that decimated U.S. manufacturing and failed the American people. Free traders promised job growth and rising living standards but it didn't happen for the majority of the middle-class, particularly workers with high school diploma or less. The free trade theology hollowed out our industrial base and instead of growth, we have decimated manufacturing industries and piled up hundreds of shortages on everything from rare earth minerals and semiconductors to cancer and penicillin drugs. We are now dependent on rogue countries like China for critical minerals, technologies, pharmaceuticals, and restrictions or bans could bring immediate harm to US businesses and citizens.

But change is coming. For the first time in decades the United States is no longer endorsing the free trade orthodoxy that resulted in the erosion of U.S. manufacturing sector. President Trump has said he wants the United States to shift to a producer economy to reduce the trade deficit, grow manufacturing industries again, and increase exports. To accomplish these goals, Trump is going to have to find solutions to the overvalued dollar, currency manipulation, and the power of the financial industry.

Strong Dollar

The U.S. dollar has been overvalued for many years against other foreign currencies. When the dollar is strong our exports are overpriced and not competitive in foreign markets. At the same time the strong dollar creates a double-digit import incentive to the great disadvantage of domestic U.S. producers. The high value of the dollar since the 1990s has acted like a massive tax on U.S. exports and a huge subsidy to U.S. imports.[1] In the last 10 years the dollar has risen in value 25.5 percent.[2]

Figure 11.1 is the CPA's Currency Misalignment Monitor. It reveals that the U.S. dollar is overvalued by 16.8 percent while our competitor's currencies are undervalued from –2 to –32.7 percent.

The three countries on the list that are most undervalued are Japan, Korea, and China which were also the top 3 surplus countries. They overproduce, underconsume, and rely on their exports for growth. The leading deficit country is the United States. The overvaluation of the dollar undermines the competitiveness of American manufacturing and agriculture. It increases the trade deficit, weakens economic growth, and exacerbates

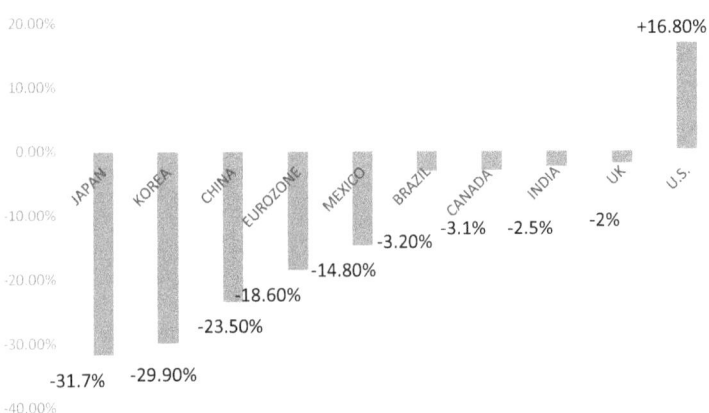

Figure 11.1 Currency misalignment monitor

Source: Coalition for a Prosperous America. Currency misalignment monitor, October 2024. https://prosperousamerica.org/Job Quality Index/

---

[1]Robert Blecker, The benefits of a lower dollar, Economic Policy Institute, June 1, 2003.
[2]Based on the Federal Reserve Board's Nominal U.S. Dollar Index (DTWEXBGS).

inequality, causes deindustrialization, and the loss of middle-class jobs. The U.S. dollar overvaluation also continues to overprice U.S. exports in the world market, making them less competitive. A recent CPA analysis found that the effect of the U.S. dollar overvaluation on American manufacturers equated to a $520 billion import subsidy for foreign goods in 2023.[3]

What Is Currency Manipulation?

Globalization and free trade opened up trade with foreign countries that engage in currency manipulation and other unfair trade practices. Currency manipulation is illegal under the rules of both the International Monetary Fund IMF and the World Trade Organization (WTO), but neither organization enforces these rules. Currency manipulation acts like an artificial subsidy for the foreign country's exports, making them less expensive, and as a tax on all U.S. exports, making them more expensive. This undercuts the competitiveness of U.S. manufacturing products which leads to trade deficits and the loss of millions of jobs.

Currency manipulation and misalignment is practiced by China and 13 other counties mostly in Asia. The way it works is that the governments (or private investors) in these countries buy up U.S. assets (such as U.S. treasuries) to increase the demand for the dollar—which makes the dollar artificially overvalued. This process makes the dollar more expensive which makes U.S. goods more expensive and the competing country's products cheaper. Most of these countries run large surpluses with the United States.

A strong currency is not necessarily in a nation's best interests. In fact, if we could reduce the overvalued dollar and balance our account we would make our exports more competitive in global markets which could spur economic growth, reduce our current account deficit, and increase gross domestic product (GDP) growth.

The Trump Administration's America First Trade Policy emphasizes identifying and taking action against currency manipulation. In June 2025, the Treasury Department put several economies on its "Monitoring

---

[3]"https://prosperousamerica.org/author/andrew_rechenberg/" Andrew Rechenberg, Currency Misalignment Monitor, Coalition for a Prosperous America, October 01, 2024.

List" to track their currency practices and macroeconomic policies, including China, Japan, Korea, Taiwan, Singapore, Vietnam, Germany, Ireland, and Switzerland. Despite Trump's America First Trade Policy, it is important to note that Treasury has not designated any country a currency manipulator and nothing has been done to stop currency manipulation.

According to economic theory, running deficits over many years is supposed to weaken our currency and eventually reduce the dollar value and reduce our deficit. The thinking goes like this: A trade deficit creates downward pressure on a country's currency under a floating exchange rate regime. With a cheaper domestic currency, imports become more expensive in the country with the trade deficit and the trade account is eventually balanced. But it isn't happening in America. We have been running trade deficits for 49 years and they get worse every year. The trade deficits get worse because our competitors manipulate currencies to keep the dollar value high.

The bottom line is that the United States has accumulated trillions of dollars of foreign debt that must be paid back in the future, either by shrinking government services or by raising taxes. According to the CPA, we shift the burden to future generations so that we can consume more than we produce.[4]

So, if currency manipulation is illegal and it makes our exports noncompetitive and really hurts American manufacturing, why do we allow it?

Why Don't We Devalue the Dollar?

Here are the primary reasons:

- The major reason is that a weaker dollar could lead to higher import costs. Higher import prices could reduce consumer purchasing power which is considered a big threat by the majority of the public.
- A weaker dollar is opposed by many U.S. companies who depend on a strong dollar and low-priced imports for their business.

---

[4]John R. Hansen, Mighty Dollar—Mighty Wrong, "https://www.prosperous america.org/america_s_trade_deficits" Coalition for a Prosperous America, August 22, 2022.

Retailers like Amazon, Walmart, and Target are examples of large corporations who want to keep import prices low and they have the lobbying power to buy Congressional votes.

- Investors, particularly foreign investors, who want to invest in U.S. assets are concerned that the decline of the dollar would not be a safe haven for investment.

- And, of course, Wall Street who sells the stocks, bonds, treasury bills and other financial assets to the rest of the world, and fear that a weaker dollar could influence interest rates, and might deter foreign investment in U.S. financial markets.

- Multinational corporations (MNCs) with plants in Asia benefit from cheap Asian labor and artificial foreign prices because they want to export back to the U.S.. They have no interest in changing the current system and want to keep the dollar strong. They use their lobbying power and political influence to forestall any attempts to legislate any solutions to currency manipulation and the overvalued dollar.

- One of the reasons that foreign countries are so willing to finance our deficit is that American tax law subsidizes it. The CPA says that other countries invest in America because it is a tax shelter. They don't have to pay any taxes on the earnings, and as a bonus, the American government avoids reporting the income to their home country tax collector. The Tax Justice Network, a London based nonprofit, says the United States ranks second only to the Cayman Islands in offering financial secrecy for global investors.

I should add that the people who have been chosen to be Treasury Secretaries for 3 decades have come from Wall Street and have always been biased against dollar devaluation in every administration. In 1994, the new treasury secretary of the Clinton administration, Robert Rubin, said, "A strong dollar is in our national interest," because it would assure foreign investors that Washington would not interfere in exchange markets to debase the currency. Since Rubin, every treasury secretary has supported the strong dollar policy. It appears that anyone coming from the financial sector, will always have the same view, which results in an anti-manufacturing policy. Trump has said he wants to turn the economy from consumption to production, but he needs to answer the question of whether he wants the economy to make money by making things or make money from money.

The government has known about currency manipulation for decades but no politician—Democrat or Republican—has been willing to face the truth and do something about it. In 2008, President Barack Obama, in a campaign appearance, said that if China continued its currency manipulation, the United States would cut off market access. And when Donald Trump was running for office in 2016, he promised that he would "declare China a currency manipulator" on the first day of his presidency. But when they got into office, nothing happened.

Currency manipulation is, by far, the most protectionist international economic policy in the twenty-first century, but, even though it is illegal, neither the U.S. government nor the International Monetary Fund nor the World Trade Organization has been willing to do anything about it.

The Financialization of the Economy

The problems of currency manipulation, the strong dollar, and the decline of American manufacturing have all been driven by the financialization of the economy. Financializaton is defined as the growing scale and profitability of the finance sector relative to the rest of the economy, and the shrinking regulation of its rules and returns

As described in Chapter 1, Neoliberal Supporters of financialization make the case that financialization is the **final or perfect form of free-market capitalism** where profits are realized the quickest, costs are minimized, and the government is not allowed to interfere in the process. Financialization is about making short-term profits and cutting costs to satisfy high-risk investors looking for quick returns.

At its peak in the mid-twentieth century, American manufacturing had 40 percent of all profits and 29 percent of the nation's jobs. The finance industry muscled past manufacturing and grew from 10 percent of GDP in 1950 to 22 percent by 2024. Manufacturing jobs declined from 19 million jobs in 1979 to 12.7 million in June 2025. Today, finance has 40 percent of profits with 5 percent of the jobs.

In his book *Bad Money*, Kevin Phillips says that starting with the Clinton Administration, both President Bill Clinton and his Treasury Secretary

Robert Rubin "saw finance leading the nation into a postindustrial era in which services, especially the lucrative financial ones, would replace manufacturing just as the latter had ushered out a shrinking agricultural sector. Finance was the next great elevator ascending into the luminous temple of progress." All administrations since Clinton have abandoned manufacturing and focused on supporting the transition to a service economy led by finance. The disproportionate growth of finance diverted income from labor to capital and reduced the number of living wage jobs for the middle class.

This financial growth has led to a tremendous increase in Wall Street's economic and political power. Wall Street banks used to finance the manufacturing capital investment and R&D that made America the best economy in the world. But after deregulation beginning in the 1980s, Wall Street became the master, demanding short-term profits over the strategies that led to long-term growth. Wall Street's demand for short-term profits forced most corporations to slim down their organizations and eliminate the functions that did not show a quick return on investment.

Financialization is about shareholder value and short-term profits and is based on speculation, risk and debt to enrich investors. It has permeated all American public corporations. It is totally about making money from money and has nothing to do with creating jobs or shared prosperity.

The argument in this chapter is that financialization and a strong dollar are not a good long-term strategy for the country or the economy. It is no coincidence that the rise of financialization has happened during the decline of manufacturing, the decline of middle-class income and capital investment, and the rise of inequality. It is also no coincidence that during the same period there was an enormous shift in wealth to the top 10 percent earners at the expense of the bottom 90 percent. It is notable that the finance industry is completely against any attempt to devalue the dollar and will lobby against it accordingly.

If Trump really supports reshoring and investment in manufacturing sectors, he should push Congress to realign the dollar, make stock buy backs illegal, and punish countries who manipulate currency with harsher tariffs or import bans.

I think there is a danger because there are limits to how long the United States can finance a trade deficit. Unsustainable trade and federal deficits can eventually can eventually lead to financial instability, potentially through a crisis. Large national debt and ongoing trade deficits can place increasing financial burdens on future generations.

So far, the United States has chosen to accept currency misalignment and trade imbalances. According to the CPA, "As a result, the US has accumulated trillions of dollars of national and foreign debts that must be paid either by shrinking government services, including social security and healthcare benefits, or by raising taxes."

Other Unfair Trade Practices

In addition to currency manipulation, there are also other forms of unfair trade by China, and other countries such as overproduction, dumping, subsidies, illegal restrictions on our exports, and the use of state-owned enterprises. China, in particular, has used these policies to develop massive excess capacity in a range of basic and advanced industries such as steel, aluminum, glass, paper, solar cells, and auto parts.

Excess capacity means that factories produce more goods than their domestic market demands. Their government subsidizes this excess capacity and expects the company to export the surplus at below-market rates (a process called dumping) and most of it is targeted at the U.S. market.

An example is the Chinese dumping of solar panels. There is considerable evidence that China has engaged in the practice of "dumping" solar panels in the U.S. market, selling them below their domestic market price to gain market share. This practice, along with allegations of Chinese government subsidies, has led to a U.S. investigation and the imposition of tariffs on solar panel imports from China and some Southeast Asian countries.

The U.S. system for enforcing unfair trade is in urgent need of reform. And we can't depend on the WTO to help us with unfair trade practices or currency manipulation. To get a ruling from the WTO requires a consent of all of the members. But it will never happen because some of the WTO members are using unfair trade practices and currency manipulation and want to maintain the status quo.

If we do nothing about the overvalued dollar:

- Eventually we will lose most of our manufacturing industries and our technologies to our foreign competitors.

- There will be no incentive for the U.S. MNCs to reduce outsourcing.
- Exports will never exceed value of imports because 70 percent of exports are manufactured goods.
- We will never reduce the trade deficit which was $1.3 trillion in 2024.
- Financing the trade deficit can't be sustained and could eventually lead to a collapse of the dollar.

If we look at the longer term, I don't see how Trump's America First Plan can work, if we can't find ways to reduce the value of the U.S. dollar, and there are many tools the government can use to achieve the objective.

Dollar Realignment

Currency realignment, or exchange rate realignment, is the process of adjusting a country's currency value relative to other currencies, often to correct trade imbalances or improve economic competitiveness. For instance, devaluing the dollar to a weaker currency can boost exports by making them cheaper for foreign buyers, while a stronger currency can make imports cheaper. Realignment of the dollar would require the approval of the President and the direct intervention of the Treasury Department. Realigning the dollar would increase our exports (mostly manufactured goods) and the agriculture sector.

Market access charge—Foreign governments manipulate our currency by buying up our financial assets to make the dollar more expensive. One way to combat this practice is by taxing purchases using a **market access charge** on all foreign investors buying U.S. assets. Over time it would begin to lower the value of the dollar to a trade balancing price. This tax would cover asset purchases including stocks, bonds, real estate, or IP—pretty much everything foreigners might want to buy, except for goods to be exported. The stated objective is to achieve a current account balance within five years.

Implementing a **withholding tax** on the profits and dividends earned by foreign investors that finance the dollar. Withholding taxes would directly reduce the net returns foreign investors receive from their investments in U.S. dollar-denominated assets, which would reduce attractiveness of U.S. assets compared to investments in other countries—eventually lowering the dollar value.

Taxing sellbacks: This is a tax on the profits of American companies who have offshored their products and sell them back to the United States. It is designed to discourage outsourcing and encourage companies to bring jobs back to the United States.

The Financial Times columnist Gillian Tett wrote an op-ed titled "Tariffs on goods may be a prelude to tariffs on money." In it, she said Washington's tariff policy could one day extend to capital flows—suggesting that "tariffs on goods may be a prelude to tariffs on money." I think this is a sign that Wall Street is waking up to the possibility of tariffs may not be Trump's final effort to stop unfair trade. Tett is correct that the next step might be using a market access charge or some kind of tax on the investor purchases of U.S. assets to realign the dollar.

The Tariff Alternative

Countervailing duties (CVDs): These are tariffs or taxes on imported goods that offset subsidies by our various trading partners. CVDs could be in the form of a surcharge, tax, or tariff. Even though tariffs have hurt some importers there is proof that they have really helped U.S. manufacturing.

The Trump administration, so far, has favored tariffs against countries who use unfair trade practices. Tariffs make the foreign competitor's goods more expensive in the United States but **would do nothing to make U.S. goods less expensive** in their countries. Tariffs are not a comprehensive answer, and what is needed is currency realignment.

"Wall Street economists and financial pundits are finally starting to admit what we've known all along: tariffs are not some inflationary monster," said Andrew Rechenberg, CPA economist.

> They like the revenue tariffs generate, but it's time they take the next logical step and recognize that tariffs drive reshoring, rebuild domestic industry, and deliver real, productive economic growth.

Tariffs are the most efficient tax the government can use, raising revenue, strengthening our industrial base, and reducing the burden of less productive, more harmful taxes on the middle class. It's a win-win, and it's long overdue for Wall Street to embrace the full picture.

It appears that the United States is avoiding devaluing the dollar for political reasons and is trying to use a combination of diplomatic pressure, negotiation, legislation, and tariffs to counter currency manipulation and level the trading playing field. But none of these efforts is going to lower the cost of our exports and make American products more competitive.

Every 10 percent rise in the dollar value adds approximately $350 billion to our trade deficit and reduces the economic activity by 1.65 percent with a corresponding loss of 1.5 million jobs.[5]

A new working paper from the CPA called "Imports Growth and Job Creation from a Competitive Dollar," reveals what could positively result if the dollar value could be reduced. The econometric model is over a six-year period and shows that the dollar price adjustment necessary to achieve a current account balance is a reduction of 27 percent. If the dollar value could be reduced this much it would result in:

1. Gross domestic product growth of 1.2 percentage points per year higher than baseline growth which is an additional $1 trillion.
2. 5.2 million additional jobs by 2024 and 1.5 million would be in manufacturing.
3. Export growth 5 times faster than baseline, while imports would grow more slowly.

In their book *Industrial Policy for the United States*, Fasteau and Fletcher make the bold claim that

Because a lower dollar will make all imports more expensive here and all exports cheaper abroad, ending its overvaluation is the

---

[5] Jeff Ferry, Chief Economist, Imports Growth and Job Creation from a Competitive Dollar, Coalition for a Prosperous America, February 2019.

single most potent tool for balancing our overall trade. Ending its overvaluation will also remove a very large headwind to almost all US industrial policies.[6]

I agree with this assessment, but does President Trump agree or does he think that he can make America First only using tariffs?

Conclusion

Neither the Trump or Biden administrations have been willing to politically take on the financial critics and do anything to realign the dollar. In July 2025 President Trump said, "I will never say I like low currency. I like a strong dollar, but a weak one makes you a hell of a lot of money." This wishy-washy response doesn't reveal whether Trump will do something about the overvalued dollar. The question of tariffs has resulted in a titanic struggle between the financial sector that wants a strong dollar and status quo, and those who want to grow domestic manufacturing. If Trump wants his America First Plan to succeed, he is going to have to choose sides. I don't think his America First Plan has much of a chance without dollar realignment.

---

[6]Marc Fasteau and Ian Fletcher, Industrial Policy for the United States. Winning the Competition for Good Jobs and High Value Industries, Cambridge University Press, 2024.

CHAPTER 12

How Will We Solve the Problems Caused by Free Trade Policies?

The only tool we have tried that competitors respond to are tariffs. So, I say again, if not tariffs what are the solutions?

After decades of deindustrialization, rising trade deficits, inequality, and 223 out of 722 U.S. regions suffering absolute declines in per capita income, it is obvious that free trade and the international trading system has failed America, and we need to seek a new path. I will make the argument that to have a chance of creating an economy with wages rising faster than inflation, and rising living standards, America must abandon free trade and globalism, bring manufacturing back to the United States, reduce our trade deficit, and protect our industries and technologies. We will also have to incentivize U.S. multinationals to stop outsourcing and incentivize both foreign and U.S. companies to establish manufacturing operations within the United States.

The Problems Caused by Outsourcing and Free Trade

Since Trump introduced his tariff solution, there has been a cry heard around the world from economists that claimed tariffs would cause a rise in inflation and an increase in consumer prices. They are saying that it would be a tax on the middle class. Their cries suggest that the only solution is to not use tariffs as a solution and return to the status quo of free trade and open markets. The argument goes like this: The United States benefits from cheaper goods and these imports reduce prices and costs for consumers so that they can buy more imports. But $4 trillion of annual imports have not delivered on the promise of substantially lowering consumer prices or on helping all of the citizens living paycheck to paycheck.

But before getting into the solutions, it is important to take a hard look at the problems caused by free trade and globalization and ask yourself what are the answers. If not tariffs, how can we resolve the following trade problems?

1. **Unfair trade and leveling the playing field**

   One of the big questions about American trade policy that has always puzzled me is why did we think it would be good for America to allow all of our trading partners cheap access to all of our industries when they won't give us the same access to their industries? A good example is the automobile industry. For instance, Japan sends 75 cars to the United States for every one car we send them. The EU charges a 10 percent tariff on imported American cars, while the United States imposes a 2.5 percent tariff on imported European cars. Europe exports four times as many cars to the United States, or 1.14 million cars per year. Our major trading partners have trade surpluses every year with the United States and force us to have trade deficits. Why should trade be so one-sided? Isn't it time to level the playing field with our trade partners, and demand fair trade instead of free trade?

2. **Shortages**—We have become dependent on imported pharmaceuticals, minerals, metals and components for weapon systems from China and other Asian countries. India and China are the leading U.S. sources for generic pharmaceuticals, which account for 91 percent of all prescriptions written in the United States.

   Mining minerals and metals are the front end of nearly every manufacturing supply chain, from smartphones and computer chips to renewable energy technologies and fighter jets. We now find ourselves reliant on imports for nearly 50 essential minerals and metals—and 100 percent reliant on imports for 18 of them.

   The United States is currently in an unenviable position where a foreign competitor could cut off our imports and really harm U.S. industries and consumers. We are victims waiting for the hammer to drop.

3. **Overvalued dollar**—The overvalued dollar causes our exports to be uncompetitive in foreign markets. China and 15 other trading countries keep the dollar over valued by using currency manipulation to make the dollar more expensive which makes our exports more expensive and the foreign countries' products cheaper. How can we stop illegal currency manipulation without the leverage of tariffs?

4. **Decline of U.S. industries**—Free trade and globalism have led to the disintegration of most manufacturing industries in terms of loss of employees and plants. Since 1980, Republicans and Democrats have watched the relentless disintegration of industries from computers and smartphones to aluminum and Class 8 trucks. So, the big question is, can the United States afford to allow our industries to continue to deteriorate until we are totally dependent on imports, or is it in our best long-term interests to protect selected industries and reshore production? If the answer is protection, then how will we do it unless we use tariffs?

5. **Innovation**—America is still counting on a strategy of innovation to compete in the future. Everybody agrees that future economic growth and international competitiveness depend on our capacity to innovate. A strategy of innovation is a noble idea, but we are losing new products and technologies through outsourcing and technology transfer agreements. If we can't reverse this trend, then a strategy of innovation is a moot point. How will we employ an innovation strategy if we can't protect our technologies?

6. **Cheating**—China uses currency manipulation, technology transfer, technology theft, dumping in foreign markets, state subsidies, state-owned enterprises, and even espionage as trading strategies. Instead of competing, like the United States and other industrial nations, they have chosen predatory mercantilism. We are in a cold war with China and the question is: How can we defend ourselves and reduce our dependency? Making a trade agreement with China without enforceable penalties for cheating is a long-term ticket to economic oblivion, which begs the question—How can we stop China and other countries from cheating?

7. **Inequality**—Income inequality has been rising since 1980. Income growth for most of the middle class has been flat compared to the

huge gains of the rich. According to Pew Research, from 1970 to 2018, the share of aggregate income going to middle-class households fell from 62 percent to 43 percent. Over the same period, the share held by upper-income households increased from 29 percent to 48 percent.[1]

According to the CPA, "One of the primary causes behind rising inequality in the United States since about 1980 has been economic globalization. As manufacturing jobs were outsourced, middle class wages declined and inequality increased." This accelerated income inequality is driven by free trade and globalization. So how will we reverse inequality as long as we outsource jobs to low wage countries?

8. **The export myth**—In 2014, President Obama set a goal of doubling exports, but it was a failure. He didn't seem to understand (or ignored the fact) that our competitors were manipulating currency to keep our dollar overvalued, which made our export prices non-competitive. Obama and many other politicians believed that free trade agreements could increase our export sales. In fact, Senator Maria Cantwell (D-Wash) said in May 2025 that "Free Trade agreements are a way for us—not tariffs—to gain the leverage we want."

She doesn't seem to understand why exports are not growing and how they are related to growing trade deficits. She, like Obama and many other politicians, have bought into the export myth and the four-decade illusion that opening foreign markets would deliver prosperity, and that the United States would get their fair share of trade. Instead of export growth, America got record trade deficits, loss of millions of jobs, and the wealth going to the top 1 percent. The only chance for export growth is to realign the dollar.

To have a chance at finding solutions to these eight problems will require getting our foreign trading partners (competitors) to change their trade strategies with the United States. But to do it will require leverage and the leverage will have to be monetary. The only tool we have tried that they respond to are tariffs. So, I say again, if not tariffs what are the solutions to these problems?

---

[1]Ruth Igielnikand. and Rakesh Kochhar, Pew Research Report, Trends in income and wealth inequality, January 9, 2020.

Other Free Trade Issues

Allowing China into the WTO in 2001—The decision to allow China into the WTO in 2001 was driven by the American multinational corporations (MNCs) who wanted to build plants and move production to China, and by politicians who supported free trade. They wanted access to the growing China consumer markets, and they agreed to technology transfer agreements that would give Chinese competitors their technologies with the additional proviso to ship their products back to the U.S. Allowing China into the WTO, was all about cost reduction by importing rather than making products in the U.S. and was supported by the Clinton administration, and free trade Democrats and Republicans. It accelerated the outsourcing of jobs and production, and has resulted in a huge increase in imports, and a run-away trade deficit.

America is at a crossroads. We must stop dealing with China as we hoped they would be, and begin dealing with them as they are. China uses a predatory mercantilist strategy based on innovative cheating using everything from dumping to espionage. We can't beat them at their game.

Congress has reviewed all of these problems and legislation to revoke China's Most Favored Nation Status was proposed by Senators Tom Cotton (R-AR), Josh Hawley (R-MO), and Marco Rubio (R-FL) in September 2024. The bill would include 100 percent tariffs on key Chinese products related to national security. As of early 2026, the probability of the Trump administration and Congress revoking China's Permanent Normal Trade Relations (PNTR) is considered high, driven by bipartisan, hawkish views on trade and national security.

The United States is in a favorable position in the struggle because the U.S. market is the largest and most important market in the world. China needs our consumer markets more than we need theirs.

The WTO Doesn't Support America

In his book *The World Turned Upside Down*, Clyde Prestowitz says that the WTO was supposed to lead to better trade rules and more order, but it failed for several reasons. It ignored currency manipulation, trade imbalances, and IP theft. Second, it has failed in effective governance because the 164 member countries must make decisions by consensus. In addition, it has completely failed at controlling China's mercantilism including state-owned enterprises, subsidies, market protections, IP theft, and so on.

The WTO has rendered itself ineffective and can no longer assure fair trade, particularly with China. Prestowitz goes on to say, "The WTO simply has no way for dealing with politically guided and coercive trade, investment, and industrial politics, any more than the IMF can deal with issues of chronic undervaluation and overvaluation of currencies and chronic trade surpluses."

Clyde Prestowitz suggests that the United States should leave the WTO and form a democratic globalization organization whose members are only democratic governments operating under the rule of law. The key members would be the United States, Canada, Mexico, the EU, the UK, Japan, South Korea, Australia, India, Brazil, South Africa, and Nigeria. It would make decisions based on weighted voting, where the larger economies would have more weight in voting. The focus of the organization would be to aim for balanced trade with no member having chronic deficits or surpluses.

Conclusion

In a *New York Times* essay in 2024, former Obama administration official Steven Rattner made a plea for the return of the United States to a global system and cited the theory of comparative advantage. Tariffs and other trade policies, he argued, "violate the principle of comparative advantage, and anyway, Americans are better off if they can buy the cheapest foreign products available." As Rattner writes:

> Every student in an introductory economics course learns about David Ricardo's 200-year-old theory of comparative advantage: the idea that by specializing in the products that they can produce most efficiently and then trading with others, nations can be better off.

This argument is a favorite of free traders and academic economists because it justifies cheap imports and running trade deficits ad infinitum. Basically, it says that nations should specialize in the things they can produce most efficiently and import the products that are more efficiently produced by our competitors. Comparative advantage might have worked in 1817 when David Ricardo described the theory, but it doesn't work for the United States today for two reasons.

First, comparative advantage does not take into consideration that unlike the nineteenth century, countries today, have very different costs. Some of our competitor's labor costs are 8 to 10 times lower than U.S. labor costs. When a high wage nation like America competes with a low wage nation like China, the choice is to either cut costs or let the manufacturing industries disappear. The MNCs chose outsourcing to low wage countries which resulted in the decline of our industries and the deindustrialization of the country.

A good example is that Canada can produce aluminum much cheaper than the United States because they have lower energy costs due to hydro power. So comparative advantage would suggest that the United States should buy all of its aluminum from Canada and abandon U.S. production. Aluminum is used in over 500 major products from beverage cans and kitchen utensils to aircraft, buildings, and electronics. It would be foolish and create more delivery and shortage problems for these 500 products if we gave up all control of aluminum production and depended totally on foreign sources—when so many U.S. industries depend on aluminum.

Second, David Ricardo didn't anticipate currency manipulation where our competitors game the system by using currency devaluation to drive up the value of the dollar making our exports more expensive and their import prices artificially less expensive. Ricardo didn't anticipate that the costs could be artificially increased or decreased.

Comparative advantage does not apply to wealthy countries like America in the modern world. Today, all of our workers and businesses are in direct competition with the low-wage world. Steve Rattner and economists use it to justify the continued importation of cheap Asian products and the rationalization of growing trade deficits. I argue that endorsing Rattner and the academic economists who support cheap imports is a race to the bottom for the middle class.

We need a proactive industrial policy that would get us off dependance on rogue countries, protect our technologies, grow our manufacturing industries and have a chance of increasing living standards. I think it can be done and will require a combination of tariffs, tax credits, quotas, selecting key industries, and adjusting the value of the dollar.

CHAPTER 13

Productivism—A Plan for American Manufacturing

Productivism is a comprehensive plan that uses tariffs, tax credits, quotas, key industries, technology protection and training.

The free trade model for the last 50 years has served multinational corporations and the 0.01 percent of income earners at the expense of everyday workers. Free trade policy favored corporate margins over citizen livelihoods. The idea that trade should be free and the dollar should float, cost America millions of jobs, and caused industry disintegration, loss of technology, critical shortages, and the destruction of families and communities. Instead of growth we got wealth concentration, inequality, record trade deficits, and wage stagnation.

An America First Trade Policy

The Trump White House report on trade said,

> For decades, the United States has shed jobs, innovation, wealth, and security to foreign countries who have used a myriad of unfair, non-reciprocal, and distortive practices to gain advantage over our domestic producers. There is no better expression of this dangerous state of affairs than America's large and persistent trade deficit in goods, which soared to $1.3 trillion in 2024.[1]

To address the many trade issues, President Trump developed a plan called The America First Trade Policy that utilizes the authorities and expertise

---

[1]Report to the President on the America First Trade Policy, Executive Summary, The White House, April 3, 2025.

of the Federal government to ensure the enduring economic, technological, and military dominance of the United States. The new America First Trade Policy is based on production not consumption.

Productivism

A new economic policy that favors production and investment is called "productivism." The term was invented by Dani Rodrik of Harvard and is a belief that measurable productivity and growth are the purpose of human organization (e.g., work), and that "more production is necessarily good."

Rodrick says,

> We are today in the midst of a transition away from what has come to be called "neoliberalism," with much uncertainty about what will replace it. If history is a guide, the vacuum left by the waning of "neoliberalism" will soon be filled by a new paradigm—and the more appropriate and adaptable that paradigm, the better. I describe in this essay an approach that I call productivism. This is an approach that prioritizes the dissemination of productive economic opportunities throughout all regions of the economy and segments of the labor force. It differs from what immediately preceded it ("neoliberalism") in that it gives governments (and civil society) a significant role in achieving that goal. It puts less faith in markets and is suspicious of large corporations. It emphasizes production and investment over finance, and revitalizing local communities over globalization. It also departs from the Keynesian welfare state—the paradigm that "neoliberalism" replaced—in that it focuses less on redistribution, social transfers, and macroeconomic management and more on creating economic opportunity by working on the supply side of the economy to create good, productive jobs for everyone.[2]

We need a trade policy that serves U.S. producers, farmers, and workers—not Wall Street, importers, and multinational corporations (MNCs).

---

[2]Dani Rodrik, On Productivism, Harvard University, March 2023.

I think the new trade policy should include strategic tariffs, tax credits, quotas, selected industries, technology protection. and training.

As America transitioned to a service economy, 65 percent of the middle class without college degrees were left behind. Most of the middle-class decline was the result of deindustrialization and Globalization. Being a technology and innovation leader is an important strategy, but is not enough to raise living standards or reverse the decline of the middle-class. I think that most politicians have awakened to the fact that we can't reverse declining living standards or solve the problems of inequality by depending on a service economy. More and more politicians are warming up to the idea that America is going to have to rebuild our manufacturing base, reshore production, reduce outsourcing, and reduce our trade deficit.

Tariffs

The Trump plan is based on tariffs which has drawn a lot of criticism from the media, from most economists, and from many citizens worried about consumer prices. The fear of rising consumer prices is legitimate, however, I think that if tariffs are implemented right (with exceptions to critical consumer products), they can rebuild our economy and really help the middle class as well as resolving the eight problems described in Chapter 12.

Trump implemented a baseline 10 percent tariff on countries not subject to other sanctions, and higher, country-specific "reciprocal" tariffs ranging from 11 percent to 50 percent on those with significant trade deficits with the United States. A study by the CPA, published in July 2025 said the 10 percent tariff "would grow the economy, adding 2.86 percent to GDP and 5.7 percent or $4,300 to real (inflation adjusted) average household income." They go on to say, "Those results are validated more accurate that other studies that make unrealistic assumptions about how our economy works."

The CPA summarizes the potential of tariffs by saying,

As demonstrated by real-world examples like the 2018 Section 232 steel tariffs, a well-implemented tariff strategy can lead to significant improvements in domestic industries, job creation, and income growth, proving to be an effective progressive policy for addressing income inequality in the United States.

Tariffs are the first step in developing a new industrial policy which prioritizes production instead of consumption.

If using tariffs to incentivize U.S. corporations to reshore products is to work, the government must convince the corporations that tariffs are permanent and that the government is in it for the long haul. To convince everybody, the government needs to develop an industrial policy with specific goals and objectives so everybody, including U.S. corporations, foreign competitors, and foreign governments, can understand the new policy.

When Trump boosted tariffs on steel and aluminum on June 3, 2025, most economists and the media warned that broad based tariffs would drive up consumer prices and inflation. The only evidence that can answer this question were the section 232 and 301 tariffs implemented in 2018 designed to protect the steel and aluminum industries and support domestic producers.

U.S. International Trade Commission (USITC) released the report, Economic Impact of the Section 232 and 301 Tariffs on U.S. Industries in March 2023.

> It took an in-depth look at the effects of these tariffs on the importing industries and on industries dependent on them…over the years 2019 through 2021. In every one of the ten industries the authors studied, the 301 tariffs led to significant increases in domestic production.

An article titled "USITC Report Shows Tariffs Boosted U.S. Production," by Jeff Ferry, chief economist of the CPA, states that the key points of the report were:

- Section 301 and 232 tariffs boosted production in all twelve of the industries studied.
- Price increases in the product categories targeted with tariffs were very small, in the 3 percent–4 percent range, contrary to mainstream media narrative.

- Most of the tariffs targeted intermediate (industrial) goods. Downstream goods, including consumer goods, saw barely visible tariff-related price increases.
- Downstream price increases due to steel and aluminum tariffs were estimated to be 0.2 percent.
- Section 232 steel tariffs unleashed a huge wave of steel investment, likely creating some 20,000 direct jobs.
- Tariffs are a valuable tool for generating growth in the U.S. economy.

The 10 countries as measured in billions of dollars, contributing the trade deficit were: China ($29.7), the European Union ($25.5), Switzerland ($22.8), Mexico ($15.5), Ireland ($12.4), Vietnam ($11.9), Canada ($11.3), Germany ($7.6), Taiwan ($7.5), and Japan ($7.4). All of these countries have a surplus with the United States every year. If the goal is to level the playing field, reduce our trade deficit, and reindustrialize the country; it is impossible to see how we could do it without tariffs.

In 2018 and 2019, President Donald Trump implemented Section 232 tariffs on aluminum, steel and iron products and Section 301 tariffs on roughly half of U.S. imports from China. America's historical use of tariffs has proved that they are useful in rebuilding domestic production. In fact, the U.S. tariffs averaged 30 to 40 percent from 1890 to 1945.

Yes, tariffs will cause problems for many businesses like big retailers and manufacturing businesses who rely on foreign imports, particularly from China. If we want to incentivize U.S. corporations to reshore products, to get foreign companies to invest in manufacturing in America, and to protect domestic industries and products, the best tool is tariffs,

I think we need tariffs for many reasons but I don't agree with how Trump is implementing his tariff plan. His tariff introduction has been crippled by stops and starts, changing time deadlines, and changes in the tariff amounts. I also think that putting a blanket tariff on a country like Canada, who is a major supplier of aluminum, auto parts, and other components used in U.S. manufacturing plants, is self-defeating.

A good example is President Trump's negotiated agreement to tariff Japanese vehicles at 15 percent. The American Automotive Policy Council says that American auto manufacturers and workers "are definitely at a disadvantage because they face 50 percent tariffs on steel and aluminum and a 25 percent tariff on parts and finished vehicles." This highlights the sticky problem of American manufacturers depending on imported parts and materials, as well as the fact that Japanese cars and parts made in Canada or Mexico can be exported to the United States at 0 percent tariff under the USMCA.

A better method would be to tariff specific industries and/or individual product classes. US Commerce Secretary Howard Lutnick in an interview with ABC News said that pharmaceuticals, semiconductors and autos will be handled with "sector specific" tariffs. He didn't define sector specific tariffs, but it sounds like industry specific tariffs. When Trump was asked about the sector specific tariffs on pharmaceuticals, he said, "Yeah, we're going to be doing that. "He said it would be in the "not too distant future. "We're doing it because we want to make our own drugs," he said.

Trump's tariff strategy seems to be to hit a country with a stiff tariff and then negotiate for a trade deal. He ruined his 2018 tariffs on aluminum and steel by negotiating too many exemptions and exclusions.

Trump's tariff strategy began with the promotion of reciprocal tariffs to force counties to lower their tariffs. I have come to the conclusion that the original idea of reciprocal tariffs will not work because of the difference in manufacturing costs. For instance, getting Vietnam to 0/0 tariffs wouldn't work because they would still have a cost advantage of approximately $3.00 per hour versus America's $30 per hour labor cost. However, I think trump's 10 percent base line tariff was necessary because it simply leveled the playing field between the United States and all other countries who have always had tariffs and value-added taxes on U.S. exports.

According to the Brookings AI Institute, "On February 20, 2026, in *Learning Resources Inc. v. Trump*, the Supreme Court ruled that the International Emergency Economic Powers Act (IEEPA) does not authorize the president to impose sweeping, open-ended tariffs—striking down the legal foundation for a central pillar of the administration's trade strategy. The decision removes the fastest tool for imposing broad country-level duties, but it does not end the tariff debate."[3]

---

[3]Brookings Institution, "Brookings Experts on the Supreme Court Tariff Decision," commentary by 19 experts, February 24, 2026, Washington, DC.

The only way to protect our industries against low wage countries like Vietnam is through tariffs or quotas. The big question is if we don't use the monetary pressure of tariffs, how can we make foreign countries compete fairly?

Key Industries

Productivism is a supply side strategy to boost the most productive industries so it is important to select and prioritize the key industries that must be protected. Table 4.2 (in Chapter 4) is a list of industries I have been following since 2001. The last two percentage columns in the table show the losses of employment and establishments since 2001.

If we are really going to rebuild American manufacturing industries using tariffs, we should begin by selecting and prioritizing industries that are vital to attaining the projected growth of manufacturing as a percentage of GDP, and industries where there are now severe product shortages because of the dependence on foreign imports. There may also be consumer goods industries that are better manufactured in countries with cheap labor, and are not vital to manufacturing growth. Some industries like textile, apparel, and furniture have lost so many plants, skilled employees, and suppliers (see page 51 in Chapter 5) and are probably not worth the investment needed to save them.

As pointed out in the introduction to productivism, it is important to select the most important industries to make an industrial policy work. Industries such as telecommunication, semiconductors, auto parts, and the ATIs have national security implications and need to be protected. There are many factors to consider in selecting the key industries, but the following are from the book *Industrial Policy for the United States*.[4]

- What is their domestic share of market?
- Who are their major foreign competitors?
- What is their national security impact?
- Is there currency manipulation by their competitor countries?

---

[4]Marc Fasteau and Ian Fletcher, Industrial policy for the United States, Cambridge University Press, 2024.

- What is their effect on potential employment?
- Potential for financing and investment

On the other hand, there are key industries vital to manufacturing growth because they serve all other manufacturing industries and the goal of increasing manufacturing's growth of all other sectors. Of these 38 industries shown in Table 4.2, I highlighted eight high skill industries because they make products or services used by all other manufacturing industries (see Table 5.1). I believe these eight industries should be protected by tariffs and receive tax rebates because they offer the special manufacturing and technical capabilities that support innovation across a broad range of industries from automobile parts and electric vehicles to semiconductors and the ATIs. Creating skilled employees who can work in these industries will also require a big investment in apprentice training.

These eight industries are important because, without their specialized capabilities and the ability to develop new processes, it will be difficult to develop new products and technologies. In the long term, the economy that lacks these capabilities or doesn't have them close to the manufacturing operation, loses its ability to innovate. This is a critical point, because it throws cold water on the idea that America can have a national innovation strategy and, at the same time, outsource manufacturing. Innovation and domestic manufacturing are inextricably linked.

Tax Credits

Productivism is also about tax credits (rebates). The Biden administration passed three major bills using tax credits:

- **The Infrastructure Bill** IIJA: The $1.2 trillion package includes a five-year allocation of $550 billion in federal investments in America's infrastructure to upgrade highways and major roads, bridges, airports, ports, and water systems. In November 2024, $568 billion (47 percent) had been spent on 68,000 projects, leaving 53 percent of IIJA funds unallocated.

- **The Chips Act:** About $30 billion in proposed CHIPS private sector investments spanning 23 projects in 15 states. These projects include 16 new semiconductor manufacturing facilities and are expected to create more than 115,000 manufacturing and construction jobs nationwide.
- **The Inflation Reduction Act:** Originally funded with $900 billion in clean energy and manufacturing investments. Under the second Trump administration, IRA funding was paused that applied to electric vehicles and also froze funding for EPA, Energy and Interior Department projects as part of a long line of executive actions that have been characterized as climate-skeptic policymaking. On July 3, 2025, Congress passed bill HR191, which rescinds unobligated funds from many of the IRA's spending programs, and in some cases, repeals the underlying programs.

The Chips Act led to big investments in new plants and equipment, in the electric vehicles, battery, and semiconductor industries. The credits have been enacted on a 10-year timescale, which gives corporate investors the certainty that an investment today will earn tax credits for years to come.

Tax credits may be more acceptable to our citizens and trading partners than tariffs and perhaps less likely to lead to retaliation. Given the huge wage differential between the United States and low-wage countries and the weakened state of our industries, both tariffs and tax credits are needed to restore manufacturing and rebuild our economy.

Representative Ro Khanna was one of the authors of the chips act and he said at a speech at Stanford University that he would like to see Chips Act for every key industry, or every industry like aluminum, steel, paper, advanced microelectronics, advanced auto parts, and climate technologies. He says, "To succeed, we'll need expedited permitting for national projects, conditional on companies paying a prevailing wage, meeting environmental standards, and not engaging in stock buy backs."

In 2023, the CPA released an analysis which found that if we could offer tax credits for all U.S. manufacturing sectors it would stimulate the U.S. economy, create 11.2 million jobs, and increase household income by 9.1 percent. Real GDP would grow by 6.3 percent and the resultant economic activity would generate $226 billion in additional tax revenue for the federal government.[5]

Tax credits beg the obvious question. How many industries can America support with tax credits like Biden did in the Chips Act?

Using Quotas

Tariffs are slowly being accepted by the citizens and politicians, but quotas might be a more effective tool for controlling imports. Quotas assign a firm limit on the volume of a specific imported product, but at the same time the government can allow in sufficient imports to meet domestic demand while the domestic key industry ramps up production. There are three types of quotas:

- **Absolute quotas** are quotas that set absolute limits on imports in volume. Tariffs aren't as predictable as quotas because countries like China can cut their export prices or transship products thorough another country.
- **Tariff rate quotas** work by allowing an imported product at a low or zero rate and then imposing a higher tariff rate once imports pass the quota threshold. In 2018 the government used this kind of tariff on Korean washing machines. 1.2 million units were allowed in a t a 20 percent tariff rate and any units beyond the rate paid a 50 percent tariff.
- **Voluntary quotas** like the agreement made with Mexico in the USMCA on steel was ineffective. It depends on the good will of the trading country and in Mexico's case, after they signed the USMCA agreement, they cheated and began shipping all kinds all kinds of steel into the United States beyond the agreed-on limits.

Simply applying a general tariff to all imported pharmaceutical supplies, including active ingredients, raw materials, and finished products coming from Europe, China, India, and Ireland, will result in higher drug

---

[5]Andrew Heritage, CPA Model Shows Manufacturing Tax Credits Boost U.S. Economy by 6.3%, Create 11 Million Jobs, Coalition for a Prosperous America, November 01, 2023.

prices in the United States and more drug shortages. Such cost increases threaten patient access to care, especially for generic and biosimilar medicines essential in oncology and other critical areas.

Using quotas and selecting specific classes of pharmaceuticals can offer greater certainty and predictability and encourage greater domestic investment in an industry than tariffs can. They are a better tool to use if the goal is to rebuild domestic industries, and for products that are shortages that we still need. Hospitals, clinics, and patients still need critical medicines now made in China or India. Quotas would be a better solution than a tariff because quotas would allow a specific number of the products to still be imported.

Technology Protection

Trumps America First Trade Policy says, "A Production Economy is a boon for innovation. Deploying trade policy tools to create incentives to reshore manufacturing will reverse this troubling trend and promote U.S. technological dominance."

However, to achieve his goal, Trump is going to have to come up with a plan to protect the technology invented in the United States. The U.S. MNCs decisions to outsource production and build manufacturing plants in Asia, rather than the United States, has given foreign competitors our technologies almost as fast as we invent them. New technologies and innovation are our only hope of competing in the world economy, but technology transfer agreements and outsourcing are giving our competitors the products and know-how to take away our markets. It is a self-defeating and short-term strategy. So, finding ways to protect our technologies should also be a part of the America First Trade Policy.

Both Democrats and Republicans whine about IP theft but say nothing about the MNCs agreeing to give their technologies to foreign manufacturers through technology transfer agreements. We probably can't do anything about technologies that are already being manufactured in Asia, but what is needed is for the Congress to assemble a list of all technologies that affect national security and put them on a "protection black list." The list should also include technologies that are part of the Made in China 2025 plan, to make it at least difficult for China to get their hands on the new technologies they need.

Of course, the question is, will U.S. multinationals cooperate with the government? Probably not for technologies that are already outsourced, but they might be interested in protecting new technologies, because there is now abundant evidence that over the long-term, transferring their technologies and manufacturing to foreign countries is a game, they won't win against unscrupulous countries like China who are dedicated to taking our technologies and replacing us as the world's superpower.

Training—Where Will We Find the Workers?

A recent study by Deloitte and the Manufacturing Institute found that U.S. manufacturing could need as many as 3.8 million new employees by 2033, and nearly 2 million of those jobs could be left unfilled. Trump's America First Trade Policy is not going to succeed without considering how we will train millions of new workers.

You can't just put an ad in the local paper to find highly skilled workers. Not anymore. You might be able to steal some skilled workers from competitors, but the pool of workers with these advanced skills no longer exists. Replacing these workers is going to take apprentice-style training, and, as Table 5.1 shows, it takes four years (8,000 hours) to make a journeyman worker from an entry-level applicant.

Labor participation rates have fallen from a high of 67 percent in the late 1990s to 62 percent today. The Job Openings and Labor Turnover Survey (JOLTS) in June 2025 shows 438,000 unfilled positions in manufacturing. Workforce shortages and skill training are critical factors in productivity growth.

In addition to the eight critical industries, I would add the need for maintenance technicians is becoming critical. If reshoring becomes a reality, I think it is a certainty that manufacturers will invest more in automation of production lines—including robots, palletizers, and a wide variety of packaging machines. The U.S. Bureau of Labor Statistics projection for the 2023 to 2033 decade indicates about 606,200 annual openings across all installation, maintenance, and repair occupations. This includes 53,000 job openings a year in Industrial Machinery Mechanics and Maintenance Workers.

There has been a tremendous investment in automation in most American manufacturing plants, which has caused a simultaneous need for maintenance workers who can maintain, troubleshoot, repair, and operate the equipment. Maintenance technicians for robots and palletizers are a good example of the needed training. They are expected to have:

- A good understanding of hydraulic and pneumatic systems
- Knowledge of electrical and electronic components, that is, photocells, switches, variable speed drives, touchscreens
- Knowledge of Rockwell software
- Knowledge of PLC and industrial computer programs
- Proficiency in electrical wiring of machines
- Knowledge of conveyors, robots, palletizers, and other packaging equipment
- Math, print reading, and electrical schematics

They are also expected to:

- Troubleshoot and program PLCs and industrial computers
- Troubleshoot electrical and mechanical components
- Weld, grind, drill, and saw
- Assemble, tear down, and reassemble automated systems

But to become a skilled maintenance technician who can operate, repair, maintain, and program equipment on an automated production line takes two years of mechatronics training and another two years of "hands-on" training to demonstrate mastery of all the skills listed above.

In most cases, the talent doesn't exist for these high skilled jobs. This is a hands-on training problem that computer maintenance software and online programs won't solve. Manufacturing is going to have to develop training that gives people the physical skills to do these high-tech jobs.

The bottom line is that America does not have enough maintenance workers in any manufacturing industry. Perhaps, it will take a tidal wave of reshoring and a national emergency to incentivize both the government and corporations to make the training investment.

The problem is complicated by the trump administration efforts to block immigration. Immigration has slowed down from 4.6 percent in 2000 to 1.1 percent in 2021, and to 0.5 percent in 2025. In the past, immigration has provided entry-level workers in manufacturing, construction, and many other industries. But until the anti-immigration movement slows down, it does not look like there will be enough entry level workers as an answer to workforce shortages in the foreseeable future.

I have reports from Deloitte and the Manufacturing Institute going back at least 25 years that projected the need for skilled workers. However, American corporations, particularly MNCs, did not favor investing in long-term training like apprentice training because of the following:

- **Outsourcing:** MNCs did not invest in the training to replace these workers because they purchased the services and products from foreign countries.
- **Time:** Most corporations did not want to invest in 8,000 hours of training per employee. Many told me personally that long-term training didn't have a good enough ROI, and their company would never invest in training that took thousands of hours to complete.
- **Cost:** Many companies also didn't support the idea of "earn while you learn" or paying the apprentice as he or she learned new skills.
- **Certification:** Companies were also reluctant to pay an apprentice to attain journeyman certification because they would have the skills to work anywhere and could leave the company that had invested in them.

Figure 13.1 shows that the United States is not investing enough in training, particularly highly skilled training like apprentice training. While the average of OECD countries is 0.10 percent of GDP, the United States invests 0.03 percent of GDP. This is a serious problem that can't be ignored if we are going to have a chance of achieving Trump's America First and reshoring program. At this point, America simply does not have enough high skilled workers in most manufacturing industries.

The reluctance to fund apprentice programs in manufacturing is revealed in the federal registered apprenticeship program. In Fiscal Year 2024, there were 679,960 active apprentices registered in the United States, and 95,000 were in manufacturing, but 95,000 apprentices are less than 1 percent of the 12.8 million total manufacturing workers. Reshoring is going to take more than 95,000 apprentices.

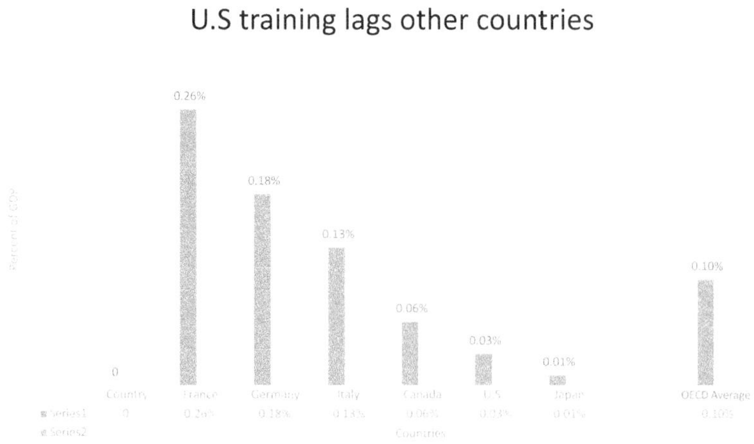

U.S training lags other countries

Figure 13.1 The United States lags wealthy nations in spending on training workers

Source: The Organisation for Economic Co-operation and Development (OECD).

Why Apprentice Training?

Commitment—Funding a four-year training program shows the company is willing to commit to manufacturing in the United States and loyalty to its workers.

Pay to learn—The apprentice gets paid for learning which means there is immediate income, that allows young people to earn a living while gaining valuable skills and experience.

Practical skills—Apprenticeships are a pathway to a skilled trade or career in specific trades or industries such as machining or tool and die, which provide practical skills relevant to the job market.

Cost—The training is focused on their career field and avoids the cost of the up-front tuition payments, and accumulating student loan debt.

Certification—Upon completion of an apprenticeship, individuals receive a nationally recognized credential, usually a certification where the apprentice becomes a journeyman, demonstrating their expertise and skills. The certificate offers job security and the potential for long-term employment.

Continued education—Some apprenticeship programs offer credits toward a college degree, allowing them to pursue further education and the potential management or supervisory jobs in the company.

If the United States is successful at reshoring manufacturing, we are going to have to train thousands of highly skilled workers and it's going to take more than a couple of community college courses or online training. What is needed is apprentice training where the student must prove that he or she has mastered each skill by proving it on the shop floor. I think it is going to take a national apprentice training program like the training programs used in World War II. It could be funded partially by tariff revenue and tax incentives to corporations.

The inconvenient truth is that, without the highly skilled workers, The America First Trade Policy is not going to work. President Donald Trump announced a workforce initiative focused on expanding apprenticeships in the United States through an Executive Order signed on April 23, 2025. This Executive Order is titled "Preparing Americans for High-Paying Skilled Trade Jobs of the Future." Trump's apprenticeship initiative has added 134,000 new apprentices but manufacturing apprentices have been minimal. The apprenticship initiative is inconsistent and contradictory and depends on the states.

The big question is financial support: At the same time as the Executive Order announcement, the administration continues to slash federal spending. Some federal funding for apprenticeship programs and apprenticeship-related research projects have been caught in the administration's efforts to downsize government and curtail DEI work. The Trump administration's proposed budget for fiscal year 2026 includes a significant cut of $1.64 billion to workforce development funding under the Department of Labor. The proposal introduces a new program called Make America Skilled Again (MASA), which would consolidate various existing workforce programs into a single block grant for states.

The DOGE website shows about $18 million in cuts to three grants issued by the Department of Labor's Office of Apprenticeship, Some grants supporting apprenticeship programs have been cut to trim costs or for perceived connections to diversity, equity and inclusion (DEI) work. The fear is that spending cuts in general could scare off employers or state agencies that might have invested in these programs.

Conclusion

Productivism using tariffs, tax credits, quotas, key industries, technology protection and training will generate economic growth, create jobs, raise household incomes, and with a forecasted one-time increase in consumer prices. But productivism also needs to be part of a Federal plan that defines the goals and measurable objectives.

Developing an Industrial Policy and Plan

The first compelling reason to develop a comprehensive plan is that our competitors have industrial policies and manufacturing plans that have allowed them to successfully export to the United States. In fact, China's "Made in China 2025" plan spells out exactly which industries and technologies they want to dominate in the future. Why can't we develop a plan that explains which industries and technologies we want to protect?

Debate about whether we need a national industrial policy is a false choice. We have a policy based on Trump's tariffs, but the current policy leaves the nation lurching from crisis to crisis and we haven't come up with long-term solutions to the economic problems that need to be overcome to make a plan work (see Chapter 14).

President Trump is making up policy as he implements tariffs. He needs to develop a plan that prioritizes manufacturing industries, defines specific tariffs by country and industry, fixes the tariff amount, and explains how we will reduce the trade deficit, stop currency manipulation, realign the dollar, and stop unfair trade and countries that cheat.

The plan also needs to specify how we will use tax credits to incentivize American companies to reshore production and how the country can use quotas instead of tariffs on products we need like pharmaceuticals.

I think Andrew Rechenberg, economist for CPA, summarizes the need for tariffs better than most economists. He said,

> President Trump's tariff proposals represent a strategic shift toward strengthening domestic production. Critics of tariff policies

consistently fail to acknowledge that the primary goal of tariffs is precisely to revitalize domestic industry and promote U.S. economic investments. By limiting foreign market share through tariffs, businesses are encouraged and incentivized to invest in American manufacturing capacity, infrastructure, and supply chains. Tariffs lay the groundwork for sustainable long-term economic growth. Far from being an economic cost, tariffs will drive long-term job creation, wage growth, supply chain stability, and the self-sufficiency of the U.S. economy.[6]

If not productivism; the alternative is to do nothing and continue to depend on free markets and the service industries with the hope that cheap imports will reduce inflation and increase living standards. Before making a judgment about tariffs, you need to ask yourself, How will America solve our trade problems without some kind of monetary leverage? If not a strategy of productivism using industry-driven tariffs, tax credits, quotas, key industries, technology protection, and training—what is the answer?

What consumers don't understand is that if we can't solve some of these trade problems, their economic future is grim. I don't think that depending on the service economy to improve living standards will work for 65 percent of the middle class. It may take some short-term sacrifice in terms of consumer prices but there is a good chance that the new productivism strategy could lead to long-term growth for the middle class.

Whether Trump's tariffs will result in economic growth, an increased share of our domestic market, and improved competitiveness is an open question. However, when you ask yourself what can we do about shortages, declining industries, loss of our technologies, and loss of our domestic market—I think readers would agree that the United States has to do something with enough power to get our foreign competitor's attention. I think the answer is a comprehensive approach like productivism that has a variety of economic methods—not just a reliance on tariffs. And the plan should include dollar realignment and stopping currency manipulation.

---

[6] Andrew Rechenberg, Wall Street's Overblown Tariff Fears Not Base In Reality, Coalition for a Prosperous America, March 11, 2025.

CHAPTER 14

Economic Factors That Must Be Considered to Make the Trump Plan Work

Returning productivity growth to its 2.1 percent long-term average is perhaps the most important challenge facing the U.S. economy and it won't happen if we depend on a service economy

I think the efforts of the Trump administration to Make America first Again with the specific objectives of reducing the trade deficit and reshoring manufacturing are admirable. But to make his plan a success he needs to also develop solutions to the following issues.

Federal Basic Research

As discussed in Chapter 7, the decline in federal basic research is not a new problem. Federal funding for basic science university research has been declining for decades. America was once the world leader in government funded research as a percentage of GDP, but has now slipped to twelfth.

An analysis by the American Association for the Advancement of Science summarizes cuts to the budgets of federal agencies and programs that do scientific research or provide grants to research universities. The association found that that the overall budget for basic scientific research would decline from $45 billion to $30 billion in 2026—a drop of 34 percent. The proposed cuts to basic research are part of a larger plan to reduce federal spending on research and development (R&D) by nearly a quarter compared to the previous year. Funding for overall science funding, which includes basic, applied, developmental work and facilities for

R&D would decline from $198 billion to $154 billion—That specific, drastic cut was proposed, but it did not happen due to congressional pushback.

The administration has framed these cuts as reducing wasteful spending, eliminating ideological bias (like DEI), and refocusing research priorities. These are reasonable goals, but the problem is that there is no easy way of determining which basic research efforts will directly translate to a new product or service. So, making arbitrary cuts to reduce expenditures could be throwing the baby out with the bathwater.

The development of new technologies into useful products is accomplished by private companies, but many of these products came, initially, from federal basic research in many fields of science. The following is a partial list of innovations funded with federal basic research:

1. *The transistor*—*invented in 1947 at Bell Labs.*
2. *First digital computer*—*invented in 1945 at the University of Pennsylvania by the Army Ordinance Ballistic Research Laboratory.*
3. *The Internet*—*invented in the late 1970s and funded by the Advanced Research Projects Agency (ARPA).*
4. *Personal computer*—*invented in 1978 with a $500,000 loan to Apple by the small business administration.*
5. *World Wide Web*—*the first commercially available browser, Mosaic, was developed by Mark Andreesen, a grad student at the University of Illinois working at its national science foundation center for supercomputing applications.*
6. *Google Search Engine*—*was invented in 1996 by Stanford computer science grad students Sergey Brin and Larry Page while working at the Stanford digital library project.*
7. *Smartphone complementary metal–oxide semiconductor (CMOS) was invented in 1992 at NASA's Jet Propulsion Laboratory at Caltech.*
8. *Solar panels*—*Bell Labs produced the first photovoltaic cells in 1954.*
9. *Nickel hydride battery*—*invented by Stanford Ovshinsky in 1993 partly funded by the department of energy.*
10. *Lithium-ion batteries invented by John Goodenough in 1980 with funding by the National Science Foundation and Department of Energy.*

11. ***Light-emitting diode (LED)***—*developed by a number of inventors and corporations that received federal funding from the Department of Energy and Air Force contracts.*

12. ***Fracking***—*The National Energy Technology Laboratory of the Department of Energy helped develop key fracking technologies, including, oriented coring, fractal graphic analysis, and large volume hydraulic frolic fracturing in 1976.*

13. ***Biotechnology***—*recombinant DNA technology enables the transplantation of genes. It was first achieved in 1973 by Herbert Boyer and Stanley Cohen at Stanford supported by NSF and NIHs.*

14. ***Automated DNA sequencing machine*** *was invented in 1986 at Caltech, by Leroy Hood and Lloyd Smith.*

15. ***Magnetic resonance imaging technology MRI***—*the underlying physics was begun in the 1950s and funded by the National Institutes of Health and the National Science Foundation.*

16. ***Artificial intelligence***—*the development of artificial intelligence began in 1956 with the Air Force funding the RAND Corporation to create the first AI program that would prove mathematical theorems.*

The cuts probably won't affect the Trump administration's near-term plans. But it is a long-term gamble, because the Chinese government is aggressively funding basic research and the technologies outlined in their Made in China 2025 plan in their efforts to become the world leader. China will probably overtake the US in science research and they want to dominate—quantum computing, artificial intelligence, biotechnology, opto-electronics, nanotechnology, advanced materials, robotics, cloud computing, the Internet of Things, electric vehicles, alternative energies data analytics, additive manufacturing, nuclear technologies, and optics. As our chief rival in the world, the question is, How can we stop them or compete with them without a growing federal science budget?

Loss of Technology Dominance

Another outcome of the reduction in federal basic research is further loss of technological dominance. A survey by the Australia Strategic Policy Institute (ASPI) called the Critical Technology Tracker is a data driven project that covers 64 critical technologies, covering, defense, space, energy, the environment, artificial intelligence, biotechnology, robotics, cyber, computing, advance materials, and quantum technologies. According to the Technology Tracker, "It provides a leading indicator of a country's research performance, strategic intent, and potential future science and technology capabilities."

The data set represents 21 years between 2003 and 2023. The Tracker focuses on the top 10 percent of the most highly cited research papers as the leading indicator of a country's research performance. In the years 2003 to 2007, the United States led in 60 of the 64 categories, while China led in 3 categories, In the years 2019 to 2023, China led in 57 of 64 categories. ASPI says, "China's enormous investments and decades of strategic planning are now paying off."

The change from American research dominance to Chinese dominance happened after China was allowed into the WTO and given most favored nation status which coincidentally began with the ongoing decline American manufacturing. China has invested heavily in science as well as a growing pool of scientists. Meanwhile, the United States faces challenges such as declining public trust in science, and concerns about the budget reduction in basic research funding discussed above.

The United States has experienced a brain drain of scientists as foreign people are educated in U.S. universities but go back to their country after their degree. The brain drain will get worse as research university budgets are cut, and scientists are forced to look elsewhere for jobs.

Again, the question is how can we stop the Chinese from technology dominance if we cut back on basic science research? More importantly, everybody agrees that America's future economic growth and international competitiveness depend on our capacity to innovate, and the key to an innovation strategy is basic science research, applied research, and R&D. So, the question is how much science research is enough, and can we stay ahead of China in science research and lead the world in innovation, if the federal budget for basic science research is reduced?

Capital investment and Stock Buybacks

Overall U.S. firm capital expenditure, relative to total assets, has been declining since 1980. Instead of increasing investments in plant, equipment, and R&D, American corporations are mostly investing in purchasing their own shares to reduce the number of shares outstanding, thereby inflating the value of the stock so they can sell it at a quick profit. In 2024, American corporations invested a record $942.5 billion in stock buybacks, according to S&P Global.

Stock buybacks beg an obvious question. Why should America's corporations reshore production to the United States. if reshoring will require higher costs such as increased building costs, transportation of equipment, hiring skilled labor, and regulatory hurdles that make domestic manufacturing less attractive than other investment opportunities; when they can make more money so much easier with stock buybacks?

Executive compensation is tied to stock performance, and CEOs are highly motivated to focus on activities that boost the company's stock price, such as stock buybacks, rather than investing in potentially longer-term domestic manufacturing projects.

Stock buybacks were once largely illegal because they were considered a form of stock market manipulation. The concern was that companies, particularly those with insider knowledge, could artificially inflate their stock prices by buying back shares, potentially benefiting executives at the expense of other investors.

But with heavy lobbying by Wall Street, the U.S. Securities and Exchange Commission (SEC) changed the depression era law in 1982 by introducing **Rule 10b-18**, which provided a "safe harbor" for companies engaging in buybacks, as long as they adhered to certain conditions.

If President Trump wants his America First project to succeed, how will he incentivize American corporations to invest in bringing production back to the United States rather than doing stock buybacks? The semiconductor companies demanded incentives to reshore semiconductor production, and received the $54 billion federal Chips and Science Act. Trump might have to offer tax incentives, loans, and grants, along with the pressure of tariffs, to get them to invest in reshoring and domestic production.

Another alternative is to use his current political power to force Congress to make stock buybacks illegal again.

Growth of Debt

Debt is the lifeblood of financialization. It is where the finance sector makes a lot of money. According to Investopedia, the total of the national debt was $36.2 trillion in May 2025.[1] The national debt is the total amount of money the country owes to its creditors.

A study by the World Bank found that countries whose debt-to-GDP ratio exceeds 77 percent for prolonged periods experience significant slowdowns in economic growth. According to Investopedia, the debt-to-GDP ratio was 123 percent in 2025. This compares what a country owes with what it produces and is an indication of its ability to pay back its debt. The higher the debt-to-GDP ratio climbs, the higher the risk of default. America is now a debtor nation sinking slowly into deeper debt, and I wonder why more people aren't concerned.

In addition, the U.S. international debt is also growing at an alarming rate. According to the Bureau of Economic Analysis, our international debt, which is called Net International Investment Position (NIIP) is the debt we owe to foreigners, which reached negative $16.1 trillion at the end of 2022. This is equivalent to 69 percent of our GDP, or on a per capita basis, $50,728 of foreign debt for each American.

Our NIIP grows as we continue to run the world's largest current account trade deficit each year. The current account deficit is made up of the trade deficit plus some smaller international flows such as investment income.

The trade deficit is the major driver of the negative current account balance. With a trade deficit of $1.2 trillion in December of 2025, the only way we can finance all those imports is by selling securities to foreigners. So, each year we increase our debt as a nation, owing trillions of dollars to foreigners. Most economists would agree that it is a sign of weakness when a nation owes more money to foreigners than it has foreign assets. This dependence on foreign imports for vital goods adds up to a grave danger to our national security.

The reason for dragging the reader through these macroeconomic figures is that, for the America First Plan to work for the long term, it will require reducing the trade deficit.

---

[1] Hiranmayi Srinivasan and Smantha Silberstein, Understanding National Debt, Investopia, May 25, 2025.

According to the CPA,

the solution is to prioritize eliminating our trade deficit, move the dollar to a competitive level, and invest in manufacturing industry at home, including plant and equipment and employee training. If we begin to invest and reduce the deficit, we will see a rise in production at home, more middle-class jobs, and more training of employees to staff these jobs. Until we do this, the NIIP will continue to grow. It is a ticking time bomb.[2]

Since the new Trump administration came into power in January 2025, they have been aggressive at cutting federal agencies and programs, which DOGE claimed is a reduction of $160 billion. However, the Congressional Budget Office (CBO) and Joint Committee on Taxation (JCT) estimate the recently passed One Big Beautiful Bill Act (OBBB), also known as H.R. 1, will increase the federal deficit by $3.4 trillion over the next decade. This is driven by $4.5 trillion in reduced federal tax revenue due to the extension of the 2017 Tax Cuts and Jobs Act (TCJA) policies and new tax cuts.

It appears that, despite a lot of talk about cutting debt and reducing government waste, the administration has, like all previous administrations, chosen to increase the federal deficit. It is important because to make productivism work and get U.S. corporations to cooperate, will require tax credits, loans and other incentives that will require government money. The question again will be, should the new plan be funded by deficit spending or should the government try to balance the budget. Every administration kicks the can down the road and avoids balancing the budget.

China Shock 2.0

Our 21 years of China trade has led to an aftershock for many communities in the United States where the loss of jobs and plants has severely affected the local economies and created economic deserts within our borders. Cities that have experienced plant closures, employment loss,

---

[2]Jeff Ferry, U.S. International Debt HAS Doubled in Five Years to over $50,000 for each American, Coalition for a Prosperous America, April 17, 2023.

and suffered from declining housing prices and tax revenue; and the rise of poverty, alcohol and drug abuse, single parenthood, and many other social ills.

The CPA is now saying that a second China Shock 2.0 is underway. Shock 2.0 is not about cheap consumer goods, but about industrial over-capacity in high tech markets and the loss of industrial products such as electric vehicles, solar panels, and semiconductors that threaten to desta-bilize economies and increase our trade deficit.

Despite all of the promises about China becoming a democratic trad-ing partner, China turned out to be a rogue trading partner controlled by the Communist Party, whose reliance on methods of cheating we ignore at our peril. They are a mercantilist predator that plays by their own rules and have created a trading game that we can't win.

What they did to the United States since 2001, they are now doing to the rest of the world. Their Made in China 2025 plan announced in 2015 aimed at dominating specific industries and technologies has been successful (it is estimated that they achieved 86 percent of their objec-tives). Their success led to overcapacity in many industries, excessive price cutting and dumping into foreign markets.

China is a fierce competitor and will do what it takes to win, in-cluding state-sponsored IP theft, smuggling, ignoring U.S. patents, government subsidies, dumping products at below-market prices, and espionage. China has evolved into the leading manufacturing country in the world by breaking the rules of the trading system which has made China a national security threat to the United States and the world.

CPA says that China invested in 700 foreign direct investment (FDI) transactions valued at $13 billion during 2020 to 2023, and that the Chinese share of Mexican exports has grown 5 percent to 21 percent since 2002. China is saying to the United States and the rest of the world, we are coming at you—try and stop us.

Transshipping to Avoid Tariffs

After Trump put tariffs on China in 2018, China began scrambling for ways to beat the U.S. tariffs. Transshipping is about shifting manufacturing operations to a country without tariffs to change the product's country of origin. China does this by using the strategy of transshipping in order to bypass the trade tariff and expand markets. The way it works is China ships parts or materials like steel to countries like Mexico, Singapore, Cambodia, Thailand, South Korea, and Vietnam. The materials are then assembled into a final product and shipped to the United States without a designation of made in China.

These countries relabel the goods or issue counterfeit certificates on the country of origin. Chinese logistics providers openly advertise "origin washing services" including reloading the shipment into a different container, altering the documents, undervaluing the shipments and misclassifying the products.

China's monthly exports to Thailand and Vietnam, in billions of dollars per month, have risen sharply in early 2025, to get ahead of U.S. tariffs. Looking at the data, it seems like China knew more tariffs were coming. This is strong circumstantial evidence that transshipments are happening.

China is also investing in Mexico to take advantage of the USMCA agreement with no tariffs on shipments to the United States. Which means manufactured goods in Mexico contain an increasing share of Chinese components, violating the USMCA content rule. This raises the likelihood that goods labeled Made in Mexico might be mostly made in China. The CPA says, "Executives of Chinese firms have admitted Mexican investment is partly driven by a desire to avoid tariffs." So how will Trump stop these illegal shipments? Will he abandon the USMCA agreement and put a big tariff on Mexico? He will have to do something because transshipping is a contradiction to the America First plan and Trump's tariffs.

China is still getting around tariffs on solar panels by transshipping them from Indonesia, India, and Laos. To defend themselves from illegal shipments and other unfairly traded imports, U.S. solar manufacturers must take on the burden of litigating, or lose the market in the process. There is a new antidumping and countervailing duty petition with the International Trade Commission in response to market manipulation, filed by the Alliance for American Solar Manufacturing, but it is unclear how the petition will be enforced.

The administration cannot stop transshipments if the tariff program is based on blanket tariffs, but if they change to industry specific like the special 40 percent tariff on Vietnam transshipping, they might have a chance. But it will probably require increasing the number of Customs and Border Protection agents in the United States.

As part of a new industrial policy of productivism, tariffs can partially help reduce the transshipping problem; but quotas are a better answer. When Mexico decided to flood the United States with steel pipe beyond the USMCA agreement, absolute quotas setting a specific number of imports would have been a better answer, than the voluntary quotas negotiated in the USMCA.

Tariffs are a better answer for overproduction and dumping because the Section 232 tariffs "establish a price floor that shields producers from the effect of Chinese overcapacity."[3] However, to be effective, tariffs must be implemented without exemptions and remain unchanged for a long period of time. This might be problematic because Trump considers himself a master negotiator and is given to changing his mind.

All of these solutions are only good if they can be enforced at the border. With China's ability to disguise shipments and bury components in other country's products, it is hard to conceive how all transshipped products can be discovered by customs and border agents.

Banning Specific Products or Specific Companies

From our 24 years of trading with China we know that there will always be some China companies who will cheat regardless of the agreement, the rules, or tariffs. When it comes to national security concerns, perhaps a better method would be to ban specific products or specific companies, like the United States did with the Chinese company Huawei.

The United States banned Huawei, citing national security concerns related to its ties with the Chinese government and the Communist Party. The core issue was the potential for Huawei's equipment to be used for espionage or surveillance by the Chinese government. This could involve

---

[3]Mihir Tersekar, How Managed Trade Can Stop the Next China Shock, The Coalition for a Prosperous America, July 2025.

intercepting communications, stealing data, or gaining access to critical infrastructure. The ban, implemented trade restrictions and limitations on equipment sales, aimed to prevent Huawei from accessing U.S. technology and potentially compromising critical infrastructure.

In January 2025, the U.S. Department of Commerce's Bureau of Industry and Security (BIS) finalized a rule prohibiting the importation and sale of certain connected vehicle (CV) technologies from the People's Republic of China (PRC) and Russia. The rule applies to hardware and software in Vehicle Connectivity Systems (VCS) and Automated Driving Systems (ADS) from entities linked to China or Russia.

Cars today have cameras, microphones, GPS tracking, and other technologies that are connected to the Internet. Through this rule, the Commerce Department is taking a necessary step to safeguard U.S. national security and protect Americans' privacy by keeping foreign adversaries from manipulating these technologies to access sensitive or personal information.

It seems that banning individual companies that have cheated (and their products), from distributing their products in the United States is a surgical and more efficient way to stop foreign competitors from cheating. Whether Trump will use the banning of companies and products as tools beyond his tariffs is unknown, but he needs to do something about the committed cheaters.

The Country of Origin Labeling Online Act

Proposed by U.S. Senators Tammy Baldwin (D-WI) and Rick Scott (R-FL) in 2023, Country of Origin Labeling (COOL) Online Act is a legislation that requires retailers to inform consumers about the origin of certain foods. This applies to specific "covered commodities" like fresh produce, certain meats, and seafood, ensuring consumers know where their food comes from. The current version of the bill (S.294) was introduced in the Senate on January 29, 2025, and is still being debated.

Business groups like the Meat processing industry, Retailer associations (e.g., Food Marketing Institute), National Association of Manufacturers), and many other business groups that support and depend on imports are opposed to this legislation. Many industry groups across various sectors have also expressed concerns about the impact of the COOL Online Act, suggesting potential negative effects on American jobs and trade relations if retaliatory tariffs are implemented by other countries.

The fact is that these importer groups are afraid of losing business if consumers can see the country of origin, particularly products from China. The fear of retaliatory tariffs is a moot point now that Trump has started a full-scale trade war with his aggressive tariff program. Companies like Amazon and Walmart lobby heavily against the COOL Act.

To achieve his goal of a "level playing field" Trump needs to make country of origin labeling a regulation for all imports. You would think that since the Republicans control both houses of Congress Trump could push them to pass the legislation.

Artificial Intelligence and Additional Energy

On July 23, the White House released its AI Action Plan, outlining the key priorities of the Trump Administration's AI policy agenda. In a speech announcing the plans, President Trump stated that the Administration's AI policies will "lead the world into the golden age of America" that will be "built by American workers," "powered by American energy," "run on American technology," and "improved by American artificial intelligence."

The AI Action Plan fulfills the core requirement of President Trump's January 23 Executive Order 14179 on "Removing Barriers to American Leadership in Artificial Intelligence," which directed the Assistant to the President for Science & Technology to develop and submit an action plan for achieving the Executive Order's policy of sustaining and enhancing America's global AI dominance. The Trump administration believes that winning the AI race will usher in an "industrial revolution, an information revolution, and a renaissance—all at once."

Artificial Intelligence will require hundreds of new datacenters to be constructed in the United States. The AI Action Plan calls for electric grid improvements for these datacenters. Specifically, the action Plan calls for a comprehensive strategy to enhance and expand the U.S. electric grid while preserving existing capacity, and embracing new energy generation sources "at the technological frontier," including enhanced geothermal, nuclear fission, and nuclear fusion energy.

Data centers use massive amounts of power for running servers, cooling systems, storage systems, networking equipment, backup systems, security systems and lighting. The industry forecasts construction of 1,357 sites in North America by 2026 requiring 64 gigawatts of new power (enough to power 56 million homes).[4]

The problem is that most utilities do not have the financial resources to build the needed generating and transmission facilities. So, the first question is who will pay for these massive energy projects? Should it be the AI developers like Amazon, Microsoft, Meta, and Alphabet? Or the customers (rate payers) of the local utility through price hikes? Or will the federal government be forced to fund the necessary generation and transmission facilities.

Second, will Trump's transition to a fossil fuel strategy be enough or will we need additional alternative energy. Trump is ending the $7,500 credit for electric cars and tax credits for solar panels, batteries, and wind turbines. Trump's domestic policy agenda will instead focus on fossil fuels as the energy solution.

I think this is a problem for several reasons. First, it is a setback for climate change supporters. According to the Environmental Protection agency, oil and gas and electric power industries are approximately 25 percent of the greenhouse gas emissions in the United States. Second, we are in global competition with China for the electric vehicle market, solar cells, and wind turbines. Losing the tax credit will put the United States in an unfavorable position in manufacturing electric vehicles, solar cells and wind turbines, and make it hard to compete. Jim Farley, the chief executive at Ford, said, "And if we lose this (electric vehicles), we do not a have a future at Ford." This is a major setback for the electric vehicle industry and a blow to manufacturing. At least 24 factories were set up to manufacture electric cars including a General Motors battery plant in Ohio.

Canceling the credit for alternative energies and electric vehicles may have given our foreign competitors these markets and is a serious (if not fatal) blow to climate change initiatives. United Nations Secretary General António

---

[4]Google. (2025). Gemini (July 2025 version) [Large language model]. https://gemini.google.com/.

Guterres called on the world's largest tech companies to fuel their data centers with renewables by 2030. But the demands for all of the datacenters is so large that it can't be done with just renewables alone, and will require fossil fuel generation. I don't think it is possible to construct all of the new data enters with just fossil fuels, but renewable generation is probably not a possibility for the time being because trump's goal is to "combat the radical climate dogma."

The U.S. Energy Department said last year that data centers already account for more than 4 percent of U.S. electricity use, which could grow to 12 percent by 2028—akin to 580 billion kWh, with AI use comprising up to 40 percent of global data-center power demand by 2026, according to research in energy journal *Joule*.

The concentrated demand from data centers will put a strain on existing electrical grids, requiring significant upgrades and infrastructure development. It could overwhelm the financial resources and operational capacity of the electric utility system, and burden homeowners and businesses with rate increases. Without the support of alternative energy, Trump's AI agenda could compromise the reliability of the electric grid for years to come.

Second, data centers also need water for cooling, and can consume vast amounts of water, with some individual facilities using millions of gallons per day. While air cooling remains common, water-based cooling is becoming increasingly important as data centers grow in size and density. This is especially true for facilities using evaporative cooling, which relies on the evaporation of water to dissipate heat. The increasing number of data centers, particularly in water-stressed regions, raises concerns about the sustainability of this water usage.

In arid regions like the Southwest, there is already a struggle between farmers and cities for water. So, it is impractical for new data centers to assume they will get enough local water now or in the future?

The Trump administration believes that winning the AI race will usher in an "industrial revolution," but if they can't do more to solve these funding, power, and water problems, the revolution might become a devolution.

Productivity Growth—A Report Card for America

The best diagnostic tool to see why the middle class declined and what it will take to recover is productivity growth.

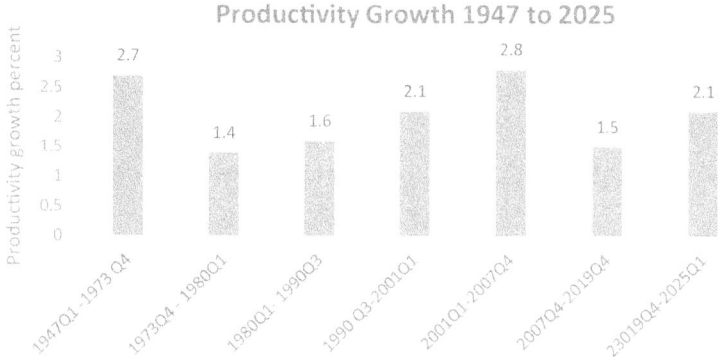

Figure 14.1 Productivity growth (1947 to 2025)

Source: U.S. Bureau of Labor Statistics.

Labor productivity, defined as output per labor hour, has grown at below the average rate since 2005. Figure 14.1 shows productivity growth since 1947 which has a long-term average rate of 2.1 percent. But since 2007, the average annual productivity growth rate has averaged 1.4 percent, well under the average of 2.1 percent going back to 1947. The government is not sure why the productivity growth is so weak, but the important factors are capital investment, income inequality, technology and innovation, education and training, foreign competition, and economic policies.

The reason that productivity growth is so important is that weak productivity growth results in low economic growth, a decline in wages and benefits, and a decline in living standards. If we are to find a solution for the declining middle class, the nation must find ways to increase productivity growth.

The decrease in productivity growth from the average of 2.1 percent to 1.4 percent resulted in the cumulative loss of $10.9 trillion in output in the non-farm business sector, according to the U.S. Bureau of Labor Statistics. This corresponds to a loss of $95,000 in output per worker. In the fourth quarter of 2021, productivity fell at an annual rate of 4.2 percent, the largest quarterly reduction in 40 years.

Productivity growth is primarily driven by technological advancements, improvements in human capital, and increases in physical capital. These factors enable economies to produce more output with the same or fewer inputs, leading to overall economic growth. So, I would argue that the overall drivers in the decline of productivity are globalization and the deindustrialization of the United States.

So, What Do We Have to Do to Improve Productivity Growth?

A positive way of looking at productivity growth, is that it is a $10 trillion opportunity if we can find solutions to the following problems.

1. **Capital investment**—American capital investment, both equipment, plant, and R&D have slowed since 2005, despite low interest rates. Investigations by the Roosevelt Institute showed that U.S. corporation capital investments decreased from 40 cents to 10 cents on the dollar in the last 30 years as corporations changed their primary investments to stock buybacks. If the trump program wants corporations to reshore their products, he will have to find ways to incentivize the needed increase in capital investments in manufacturing and the reduction of stock buybacks.

2. **Education and skills**—Several years ago when I was in Washington, DC, I visited the National Association of Educational Progress (NAEP) because I wanted to find out about the high school students test results. I was startled to find out that in math, science and reading only 24 percent of all high school graduates were proficient in the year 2019—which means 76 percent of the students were not proficient. I don't know what is going on with high school education systems, but we're not graduating the students that can compete in our global competition with foreign countries. One solution is to give up on the "everyone should go to college" standard and develop a new system that emphasizes skills and the trades.

   Another problem is that most high school students don't pursue STEM (Science, Technology, Engineering, and Mathematics) courses. They view STEM as too difficult, there is a lack of interest, inadequate preparation, and for many schools there is a limited access to STEM courses. Additionally, some students are discouraged by the perceived lack of career opportunities or the demanding nature of STEM fields.

If we can't change these problems at the high school level, it will seriously affect our efforts to increase productivity growth.

3. **Workforce shortages**—America is not ready to reshore production because we are facing serious workforce shortages in almost all manufacturing industries. In most cases, the talent doesn't exist for these high skilled jobs. Manufacturing is going to have to develop training that gives people the physical skills to do these high-tech jobs. Perhaps, it will take a tidal wave of reshoring and a national emergency to incentivize both the government and corporations to make the training investment. If we can't reduce workforce shortages, it will have negative effect on productivity growth.

4. **New technologies and innovation**—These are key factors in productivity growth described above. The ASPI tracker reveals that the United States used to lead in 60 of 64 science subjects, but has lost this lead to China which now leads in 57 of the 64 science factors. At the same time, federal basic science research has been declining for decades. These two factors will have a serious impact on technology and innovation as they apply to productivity growth. Basic research is a many faceted subject, and it is hard to identify the best technologies. But if we want to improve our technology and innovation position on the world stage and boost productivity growth it will require a larger investment in basic science research. It is counterintuitive that instead of investing in science research and innovation the Trump Administration reduced the overall science budget for 2026 by 34 percent.

5. **Economic policies**—The economic policies of the government going back to the Reagan administration in the 1980s have been supportive of free trade, globalism, imports, and the increase of trade deficits. These economic policies led to free trade agreements like NAFTA, which cost thousands of American jobs and the transfer of plants and production to Mexico and Canada. They also led to the acceptance of China into the WTO, which led to 3.4 million lost jobs between 2001 and 2017 according to the Economic Policy Institute. It is obvious that these economic policies did not favor the middle class, and, in fact, pushed millions of workers into lower paying jobs and declining living standards. Economic policies since 1980 have not favored the middle class or productivity growth.

Economic policies that lead to rising or declining living standards are critical to productivity growth. The question is, will the new trump economic policies lead to increasing living standards for the middle class, or will the top 10 percent of earners receive most of the gains?

6. **Foreign competition**—The free trade policies of the last four decades allowed our foreign competitors to gain a competitive advantage over the US using low labor costs, tariffs, value-added taxes, currency manipulation, unfair trading practices; and the government did nothing to stop them. President Trump is the first administration to attempt to level the playing field and reduce their competitive advantage with his tariff program. Reducing our competitive disadvantage is crucial to improving productivity growth.

7. **Income inequality**—The factors that contributed to increasing inequality described in Chapter 1 included free trade, globalization, and the rise of neoliberalism. They turned out to be an inequality trap where the average middle-class citizen bore the brunt of the economic crisis through job losses, stagnant wages, and not being able to keep up with inflation. Not since the Gilded Age have the wealthy accumulated so much wealth leading to so much inequality and misery for the middle class. I do not see any chance that the problem of inequality and declining living standards can be solved if the United States continues to pursue free trade policies and depends on the service sector of the economy. I think our only chance is to change the economy from consumption to production and trump's agenda is our only hope.

8. **Automation**—Automation in manufacturing is another way to achieve productivity growth. Over the last 50 years, America has been successful in automating plants using robots, palletizers, automatic packaging machines, computers, and a wide variety of programming and digital advances. Automation has demonstrably contributed to productivity growth in the United States and is expected to continue to do so in the future by increased efficiency and speed; reduced errors, improved quality, reduction of labor costs; and minimized expenses associated with errors and rework. By taking over repetitive tasks, automation has allowed employees to

concentrate on more complex, creative, and strategic activities that demand human skills and judgment.

However, the downside is that automation also displaces workers which increases income inequality. Moving to another manufacturing job, may require new worker skills, which has led to challenges in finding and training workers. Automation can unevenly distribute the costs and savings by exacerbating income and wealth inequality.

Conclusion

Trump administration's plan to use tariffs has many flaws and is not a comprehensive plan that could change the economy from consumption to production. But his administration deserves credit for being the first administration, Republican or Democrat, that has described all of the problems caused by globalization and free trade, and has been willing to take action and try to do something about it. He recognized that over the decades all of our competitors had been allowed by us to gain unfair advantage in trade while the government did nothing to stop them. And he did something about it using tariffs, while the mainstream media and economists have cried loudly about the danger of tariffs without offering their own solutions.

Returning productivity growth to its 2.1 percent long-term average is perhaps the most important challenge facing the U.S. economy. Success could deliver prosperity to the middle class, improve living standards, give workers better jobs, and reduce inequality. Whether Trump's plan to change trade will eventually lead to increasing productivity growth is an open question, and looks doubtful sat this time.

CHAPTER 15

Refloating the Boats: What Do We Have to Do to Grow the Middle Class?

I think it is possible to grow the middle class, increase wages, and improve living standards and income for much of the middle class if the country can commit to production, not consumption.

Neoliberalism is an ideology that emphasizes globalism, free trade, privatization, and deregulation. The idea emerged in the mid-twentieth century, and became a US economic policy when multinational corporations (MNCs) and the government adopted globalism and began outsourcing to low-cost countries in the 1970s. Neoliberalism is not a program based on economic theory: It is political agenda based on free markets where there are definite winners and losers.

Milton Friedman was one of the founders of neoliberalism and he became famous when he said in *The New York Times* article that "An entity's greatest responsibility lies in the satisfaction of the shareholders." The doctrine of shareholder value put neoliberalism and globalism into overdrive as a new business philosophy for American MNCs and the government. It would have dire consequences for labor, unions, workers, and communities and would be the driving force in the economy from 1980 to the present.

Neoliberalism was about efficiency and cost reduction. It was supposed to reduce costs through privatization, deregulation, offshoring, and the reduction of unions, wages, taxes, pensions and government welfare programs. It also promoted the acceptance of monopolies as indictors of greater efficiency.

In Chapter 2 I said,

> Globalization and the rise of neoliberalism as a political ideology turned out to be a trap where the average middle-class citizen bore the brunt of the economic crisis through job losses, stagnant wages, and not being able to keep up with inflation. At the same time, not since the Gilded Age have the wealthy accumulated so much wealth leading to so much inequality and misery for many in the middle class.

Globalism and the Decline of the Middle Class

Regression to the Mean (RTM)—As described in Chapter 2, RTM, was perhaps the most critical factor in the decline of the middle class. It pitted American workers against low wage workers around the world, and over time reduced American wages closer to the mean of foreign wages—which led to wage stagnation.

According to Jeff Ferry of the CPA,

"The strength of our manufacturing sector from 1870 to 1970, and its tendency to pay high wages to its workers was the single most important factor in national wealth and in our strong middle class. The aim of globalization from 1990 on, was to force US workers to compete with low wage workers around the world."

Stagnant Wages—Since 1973, hourly compensation of the vast majority of American workers has not risen in line with economywide productivity. Net productivity grew 80.9 percent between 1979 and 2024. Yet inflation-adjusted hourly compensation of the median worker rose just 29.4 percent, over this same period. Productivity has grown 2.7 times as much as pay. Which left wages for most workers flat.

Real Wage Trends—The inflation-adjusted wage trends in Table 15.1 from 1979 to 2018 shows that worker's wages with a high school education or less have declined in real terms in the top, middle, and bottom of the wage distribution. According to the Economic Policy Institute, 65 percent of the workforce do not have a college degree.[1] This is 107 million workers. Wage gains are the primary lever for raising living standards.

---

[1] Robert E. Scott and David Cooper, Almost two-thirds of people in the labor force do not have a college, Economic Policy Institute, March 30, 2016.

Table 15.1 Real Wage Trends from 1979 to 2018

Education Group	10th percentile	50th percentile	90th percentile
High school or less	−3.7%	−12.7%	−9.7%

Source: Bureau of Labor Statistics, Occupational Employment and wage statistics.

Rising prices—Today, millions of middle-class citizens are worried about rising prices and inflation as was evident in the 2024 election when they voted their pocketbook. The result of this wage trend is declining middle class income and people living paycheck to paycheck. According to the Lending Club, 64 percent of U.S. consumers (115 million) were living paycheck to paycheck in December 2022, up 3 percentage points from 61 percent the year prior. "The effects of inflation are eating into every American's wallet and as the Fed's efforts to curb inflation drive up the cost of debt, we are seeing near record numbers of Americans living paycheck to paycheck," said Anuj Nayar, financial health officer at Lending Club."[2]

Trump promises—In response to this growing public outcry about rising prices, Candidate Trump made the following promises to consumers during his campaign for the Presidency:

1. "Starting on day one, we will end inflation and make America affordable again, to bring down the prices of all goods" (NBC Montana, *Trump Rally in Bozeman, MT* [August 9, 2024]).
2. "Under my administration, we will be slashing energy and electricity prices by half within 12 months, at a maximum 18 months."
3. "Starting the day I take the oath of office, I will rapidly drive prices down and we will make America affordable again. We're going to make it affordable again" (PBS NewsHour, *Trump speaks at campaign rally in Wilkes-Barre, Pennsylvania* [August 17, 2024]).
4. "We will eliminate regulations that drive up housing costs with the goal of cutting the cost of a new home in half. We think we can do

---

[2]Anuj Nayar, Financial Health Officer, 9.3 Million More U.S. Consumers Ended 2022 Living Paycheck to Paycheck Than in 2021, Lending Club Corporation, San Francisco, CA, January 30, 2023.

that" (NBC News, *Trump Addresses Economic Club Of New York*, YouTube [September 5]).

5. "We're going to get the prices down. We have to get them down. It's too much. Groceries, cars, everything. We're going to get the prices down. While working Americans catch up, we are going to put a temporary cap on credit card interest rates at 10 percent. People are being made to pay 25 percent. Temporary ban" (*Speech: Donald Trump Holds a Campaign Rally in Erie, Pennsylvania*, Roll Call [September 29, 2024]).

6. "Starting on day one, we will end inflation and make America affordable again. We'll do that. We've got to bring it down" (PBS NewsHour, *Trump delivers campaign remarks in Waunakee as vice presidential debate set to begin*, www.youtube.com/watch?v=3Xy TEAGiNnA [October 1, 2024]).

7. "A vote for Trump means your groceries will be cheaper" *Former President Trump Campaigns in Pittsburgh*, C-SPAN (November 4, 2024).

These public promises may have set the Trump administration up for failure if consumer prices continue to rise significantly. Trump is known for making bold promises, but promises to drive consumer prices down at the same time he is launching massive tariffs could derail support for Trump's America First strategies and also affect future elections if prices climb steeply. The threat that tariffs will raise consumer prices and be a tax on every citizen is a legitimate claim, although the exact amount per citizen is still up in the air because the tariff plan is still being invented.

The Trump administration has shown that it can issue sector specific tariffs, like it has done with pharmaceuticals, semiconductors, steel, and aluminum—as opposed to blanket tariffs on countries. So, they have the option to use this selective power to exclude or exempt tariffs on specific consumer products and focus the tariffs on industrial products and technologies. For instance, Trump may find that exemptions are necessary to exclude certain cancer drugs from a general tariff on pharmaceuticals which are badly needed in the United States. So why not exempt many consumer products sold at big retailers like Walmart and Target that people buy every day. This could reduce the threat of price increases to consumers and give Trump's tariff program some positive promotion.

Winners, Losers, and Inequality

Income inequality—The primary cause of rising inequality is economic globalization, free trade, and the RTM. From 1970 to 2018, the share of aggregate income going to middle-class households fell from 62 percent to 43 percent.[3] Over the same period, the share held by upper-income households increased from 29 percent to 48 percent.

Losers—For those left behind in the new system, there is a feeling of powerlessness. The primary problem is that the system now supports the minority with no regard for the majority. Deindustrialization and globalization have led to the decline of the middle class, and sacrificing jobs, industries, technologies, suppliers and communities.

This is important because I believe that the number one threat to constitutional government is the continued decline of the middle class.

Winners—On the other hand, free trade has been very good for the rich. The big beneficiaries are primarily those who own or invest in international trade and take advantage of reduced trade barriers. A Harvard University study said, "we conclude that the import channel is the dominant force linking trade to earnings inequality, with the largest gains from trade occurring at the top of the income distribution."[3]

The Postindustrial Service Economy

Many economists and academics have convinced themselves that the transition to the service economy is a good and inevitable thing. Steve Ratner, served as counselor to the Treasury secretary in the Obama administration, said in a June 2025 NY Times article that, "We derive enormous benefits from importing goods at far less cost than we could make them

---

[3]Kirill Borusyak and Xavier Jaravel, 2022, "Imports, Exports, and Earnings Inequality: Measures of Exposure and Estimates of Incidence," *The Quarterly Journal of Economics.*

for here."[4] Economists like Ratner, believed that the service economy and cheap imported goods would provide economic growth, good jobs, and improved living standards for the middle class.

When economists, consumers, and the media all say they don't want tariffs, I think it implicitly says they would like to maintain the status quo, eliminate all tariffs and trust in the post-industrial service economy and cheap imports (rather than manufacturing sector) to improve living standards. The United States has been transitioning to the service economy and dependent on cheap imported goods for decades, but, as Table 15.1 shows, rising living standards just didn't happen for millions of workers.

The big question is … If the transition to a service economy was such a good idea, why are so many people unhappy with their income and living standards and fearful of the future? *Why are most people in America concerned with affordability and rising prices. The fact is that the transition to the post-industrial service economy did not work for most citizens and did not raise living standards.*

My contention is that continuing on the service economy path won't solve our economic problems or reverse the decline of the middle class. America needs to find a different path if we want to change the economy to an economy that works for everyone.

Also, continuing on the service economy path is not going to solve the eight problems described below.

The Eight Problems Caused by Free Trade Policies

If we don't use tariffs to force our competitors to trade fairly, how we will solve the following trade problems described in Chapter 12:

- **Shortages**—Outsourcing and the hollowing out of our industrial base, also led to shortages of everything from rare earth minerals and semiconductors to antibiotics and cancer drugs.
- **Overvalued dollar**—Currency manipulation is a financial tool used by China and 13 other countries, mostly in Asia, to make

---

[4]Steve Ratner, June 6, 2005, Manufacturing Jobs Are Never Coming Back, New York Times.

the dollar artificially more expensive, which makes U.S. exports more expensive and the competing country's products cheaper.

- **The export myth**—The fact is that we have no chance for export growth with an overvalued dollar,
- **The decline of manufacturing industries**—Can the U.S. afford to allow our manufacturing industries to continue to deteriorate until we are totally dependent on imports?
- **Cheating**—How can we stop our foreign competitors like China from cheating? Specifically, what leverage do we have if we don't use tariffs?
- **Inequality**—With the collapse of manufacturing many of the workers had to take jobs in lower paid industries like leisure and hospitality and retail. How will we improve inequality and living standards if we continue to depend on a service economy?
- **Unfair trade barriers**—One wonders how did the United States ever allow all of our trading partners to impose tariffs and value-added taxes of 10 to 50 percent against the United States over the last six decades, and did nothing to reciprocate.
- **Innovation strategy**—Innovation comes from R&D, and 70 percent of R&D comes from manufacturing. How can we be the leader in innovation unless we can grow our manufacturing sector?

None of these problems will be solved if America continues with the status quo, and reliance on a service economy, free trade, and an economic policy based on cheap imports. To have a chance at finding solutions to these eight problems will require getting our foreign trading partners (competitors) to change their trade strategies with the United States. But to do it will require leverage and the leverage will have to be monetary.

I think most readers will agree that the United States has to do something with enough leverage to get our foreign competitor's attention. The only tool we have tried that they respond to are tariffs. But the real answer is a comprehensive approach like productivism that has a variety of economic methods—not just a reliance on tariffs. And any plan or policy should include dollar realignment and stopping currency manipulation.

To have a chance of creating an economy with wages rising faster than inflation, and rising living standards, my argument is to abandon globalism and dependance on the postindustrial service economy and consumption, and focus on production, reshoring, and using tariffs to protect key industries and technologies—with the primary goal of reducing our trade deficit.

The Trump administration is betting that tariffs will incentivize U.S. multinationals to stop or reduce outsourcing and incentivize both foreign and U.S. companies to establish manufacturing operations within the United States. The new economic policy could improve the middle-class share of income and reduce the rise of populism.

The debt crisis

J P Morgan warns that the $38 trillion national debt and the $1.2 trillion dollar interest could push economic stability to the edge. The debt crisis is not down the road -it is here. I think the economy is at a dangerous inflection point. The nation is spending 40% more than it is taking in, and America is slowly going broke.

The U.S. debt-to-GDP ratio has been above 77% continuously since 2009. The higher the debt to GDP ratio climbs, the higher the risk of default.

The inconvenient truth is that deficits are a significant head wind that could undermine manufacturing reshoring and the America First Program. This financial crisis begs the question of whether America can afford to fund Trump's America First Program and the subsidies, and tax credits it will take to get American corporations to reshore their production. The capital investments for innovation have disappeared in the last 30 years and were replaced by stock buybacks. It will take a lot of investment to execute an innovation strategy.

Some financial people believe that deficits do not matter and that government debt differs from private debt, because government can issue its own currency and can create the money to meet its obligations. This is "magical thinking" that could lead to the economy going off the cliff like it did in 2007.

If we want to change the economy from a consumption to a production economy and give hope to the middle-class, we are going to have to face our financial problems and focus on a goal of reducing the debt to

GDP ratio to 70%, and a sustained multi-pronged strategy to reduce federal deficits.

The simple answer is that we will have to raise tax revenue and cut spending. Social Security, Medicare, Medicaid, and Defense comprise 60 to 70% of federal spending . Reforming these programs is a necessary condition for fiscal health, which could include measures like: readjusting benefits, raising retirement ages, allowing Medicare to negotiate drug prices, reducing defense spending, broadening the tax base by eliminating itemized deductions, introducing a national value-added tax (VAT), increasing corporate tax rates, increasing top income tax rates for high earners (including the 1%), and raising the cap on earnings subject to Social Security payroll taxes.

The Trump's solution to the debt crisis of reforming federal programs by the eradication of waste and fraud has saved only $80 billion. The savings generated are relatively small amount compared to the federal deficit or interest on the deficit. In addition, the administration extended the Tax Cuts and Jobs Act which will increase the deficit by$3.4 trillion over the 2025-2034 period.

A long-term commitment and a bipartisan consensus among policymakers are crucial to making these difficult changes, and there will be resistance from all levels of society. But if we are to have a chance at developing programs that will really help the middle class and the economy in the long run, we must first get our financial house in order. It will be hard, painful, and political, but is a problem we must face. Because ignoring the problem and depending on deficit spending will only postpone the economic engine going off the tracks in the future.

The hard truth is that government at all levels, consumers, and politicians will have to accept that austerity is the road to stability and ultimately to prosperity

What was Good for Multinational Corporations (MNCs) Was Not Good for America

The interests of U.S. multinationals and the interests of the country have diverged. The last 45 years have been very hard on American manufacturing, workers, citizens, communities and the country. A large part of the responsibility for what has happened to the middle class can be attributed to America's multinational corporations (MNCs).

The Business Roundtable is an association of CEOs from America's leading companies. Essentially, it's a lobbying group that represents the interests of major American businesses in Washington, DC. In 1997, the Business Roundtable issued a statement that said, "the point of a business enterprise is to generate economic returns to its owners, period." And so, shareholder value and short-term profits became the driving force at the long-term expense of employees, communities, the economy, and country.

In August 2019, 181 CEOs signed a commitment letter to lead their companies not just for the benefit of their investors, but "for the benefit of all stakeholders: customers, employees, suppliers, communities, and shareholders." Jamie Dimon, CEO of the Wall Street firm J.P. Morgan Chase, commented that

> the American dream is alive, but fraying. Major employers are investing in their workers and communities because they know it is the only way to be successful over the long term. These modernized principles reflect the business communities' unwavering commitment to continue to push for an economy that serves all Americans.

In my opinion, the only way they can reach their new goals and keep their pledge to help employees, communities, and suppliers, and an economy that serves all Americans is to back away from their "shareholder only" and outsourcing model and begin reshoring production. But so far, they are not walking their talk. It looks like U.S. MNCs are willing to operate for all stakeholders only if it doesn't interfere with stock prices and profit.

U.S. MNCs and Wall Street have had the nation by the throat for many decades and have dictated the future of the middle-class living standards. In fact, they are going to have to be forced to live up to their pledge. The Trump tariffs may be the first step in making them walk their talk and to honor their pledge. U.S. MNCs understand the monetary pressure of tariffs and the rising costs of importing products and materials from foreign countries.

Cyclical Theory

Historically, it seems that the ups and downs between the rich and poor is cyclical. The wealthy citizens seem to get the upper hand but then are stifled by some downturn in the economy. A good example was the Gilded Age, where the wealth and power of the very rich carried into the 1920s. But then came the crash of 1929, the Great Depression, and the New Deal, which brought reform, higher taxes, and progress for the average worker. This prosperity for the middle class lasted until 1980 when neoliberalism became the driving force and the middle class began its long decline.

Neoliberalism was a 180-degree reversal from Keynesian economics used in the New Deal, which was the first government program to establish a minimum wage, maximum hours, protecting the right to unionize and bargain collectively through the National Labor Relations Act, creating a social safety net with the Social Security Act to aid the elderly and unemployment insurance for workers.

The Country Comparison

In his book *Bad Money*, Kevin Phillips argues that a strong financial sector, or "financialization," did not prevent the decline of major powers like Spain, the Dutch Republic, and the British Empire, as their manufacturing bases diminished. Spain in the seventeenth century, Holland in the eighteenth century, and Britain in the nineteenth and twentieth centuries were all manufacturing power houses and leaders of the world economy but their economies shifted to financialization and the strong financial sector failed to sustain national power when the manufacturing and productive base waned.

Phillips says, "No previous leading world economic power has enjoyed a full-fledged manufacturing renaissance after becoming unduly enamored of finance." He suggests that this shift leads to an economy dominated by financial speculation, high debt levels, corporate venality, and corrupted politics, which can ultimately undermine national strength. In regard to banking and financialization, Phillips says, "Banking is not the creation of our prosperity, but is the creation of it. It is not the cause of our wealth, but is the consequence of our wealth."

This thesis suggests that the focus on generating wealth through financial services and debt products, rather than the production of goods, creates an unsustainable economic model that ultimately leads to instability and decline. Phillips argues that the United States is mirroring the historical pattern of Spain, Holland, and Britain. He sees similarities like the preoccupation with finance, technology, and services over basic manufacturing; the prevalence of speculation and economic bubbles; the outsourcing of capital and jobs; the reliance on foreign labor; and growing wealth inequality.

The finance industry muscled past manufacturing to become the largest sector of the U.S. economy, and the problem today is that Wall Street is no longer interested in financing long-term real investment, particularly the investment in capital projects and R&D in the manufacturing industries. Investment in financial assets is crowding out investment in real assets because the pressure is for quick returns and stock buy backs. The success of the finance industry is based on growing indebtedness and the use of financial engineering tools that redistributes wealth rather than creating new wealth.

I think counting on financialization and a service economy instead of manufacturing is a house of cards that will crash and America will decline like Spain, Holland, and Britain did unless we can get back to a production economy and real investment that leads to long-term growth. Left to their short-term profit strategies, inequality will worsen, manufacturing will not grow, GDP growth will remain low, the federal debt will continue to grow, and the potential for financial crashes will be high.

The China Plan and a Long-Term Strategy

China knew that American corporations would chase low costs around the world to enhance short-term profits. Once American manufacturers were hooked on low prices and outsourcing, China knew they would get our products, technology secrets, and eventually whole industries. It was a brilliant strategy because once they had the products, they could use our dependance to choke and dominate America in many different ways. It is all part of the globalization trap.

An objective observer might interpret the pursuit of low wages around the world and giving our foreign competitors our technologies as American capitalism sowing the seeds of its own destruction. In abandoning American manufacturing and pursuing short-term profits and shareholder value over all other considerations, they may be ceding their number one position in the world economy to China.

Globalization Is Fracturing

Globalization is fracturing, meaning the world economy is splintering into distinct blocs, rather than a single, interconnected network. This fracturing is driven by the implementation of Trump's tariffs, political instability, the rise of protectionist policies, reactive tariffs by foreign competitors, and geopolitical tensions, which are dividing the globalized world into separate trading blocs. The United States–China trade war, the pandemic, and the war in Ukraine have also accelerated the fracturing of this globalized system.

The fracturing of the global economy has led to slower economic growth, increased protectionism, and disruptions to supply chains, but it can also give the United States some big advantages such as tariff revenue, reshoring of manufacturing and the potential for reduced trade deficits.

Refloating the Boats

From 1940 to 1980 the growth of the middle class increased with productivity growth and all boats rose with the tide. The old adage "a rising tide lifts all boats" used to apply to the American economy. It used to mean that good economic policy could grow all sectors of the economy which would raise the living standards of all Americans. It was a time when the American Dream was truly attainable by any American worker with determination.

This old adage has a new meaning in the economy of the twenty-first century where globalization and financialization are the rule, and fewer boats are rising with the tide. This ocean parable begs the question, is it still possible for the average worker to attain the American Dream and can the decline of the middle class be reversed? I didn't think so for many years as the big importers and the outsourcing corporations were totally in charge. But then came Trump to upset the applecart with his tariffs and bold promises. Trump's tariffs are only a first step in using tariffs to level the trading playing field and protecting our manufacturing industries and technologies.

I think it is possible to grow the middle class, increase wages, and improve living standards or income for much of the middle class if the country can commit to production, not consumption, and use the elements of productivism to develop a comprehensive plan.

Bibliography

Case Anne, and Angus Deaton. 2020. *Deaths of Despair and the Future of Capitalism.* Princeton University Press.

Fasteau, Marc, and Ian Fletcher. 2024. *Industrial Policy for the United States.* Cambridge University Press.

Hartmann, Thom. 2022. *The Hidden History of Neoliberalism, How Reaganism Gutrted America and How to Restore Its Greatness.* Berrett -Koehler Publishers, Distributed by Penguin Random Houe Publishers.

Hartmann, Thom. 2024, *The Hidden History of the American Dream.* Berrett -Koehler Publishers, Distributed by Penguin Random Houe Publishers.

Kiernan. Peter D. 2015. *American Mojo Lost and Found, Restoring Our Middle Class Before the World Blows By.* Turner Publishing Company.

Kurlantzick, Joshua. 2013. *Democracy in Retreat, The Revolt of the Middle Class and the Worldwide Decline of Representative Government.* Yale University Press.

Leicht, Kevin T., and Scott T. Fitzgerald. 2023. *Middle Class Melt Down in America*, Routledge.

Lighthizer, Robert. 2023. *No Trade Is Free.* Harper Colins Publishers.

Rising Above the Gathering Storm Committee (U.S.), National Academy of Sciences, National Academy of Engineering, and Institute of Medicine. 2010. *Rising Above the Gathering Storm, Revisited.* The National Academies Press.

Rodrik, Dani. 1997. Has Globalization Gone Too Far. Institute for International Economics.

Waddell, William. 2024. *Reclaiming American Manufacturing, Take Back the Middle Class from Globalism.*

About the Author

Michael Collins has 35 years of experience in manufacturing. Before retiring in 2004, Collins was vice president and general manager of two divisions of Columbia Machine in Vancouver, Washington. Their major customers were the S&P 500 multinational corporations, and he worked with them from 1974 to 2004. This experience gave him a firsthand look at America's multinational corporations and their strategies. He was able to watch firsthand the beginning of outsourcing and the focus on short-term profits and shareholder value.

He has written for many industrial trade journals, including *IndustryWeek*, *Forbes Magazine*, Industrial Equipment News, and Manufacturing.Net. Since September 2007, he has written and published more than 460 articles and columns on a wide variety of topics.

He is also the author of the following five books:

1. *The Manufacturers Guide to Business Marketing* (1994)
2. *Saving American Manufacturing* (2006)
3. *Growth Planning Handbook for Small and Midsize Manufacturers* (2006)
4. *The Rise of Inequality and the Decline of the Middle Class* (2016)
5. *Dismantling the American Dream—How Multinational Corporations Undermine American Prosperity* (2022)

He holds an MBA from City University and a BS degree from Portland State University in Portland, Oregon.

Index

www.ingramcontent.com/pod-product-compliance
Lightning Source LLC
Chambersburg PA
CBHW061506180526
45171CB00001B/55